A JESUS SHAPED LIFE

DISCIPLESHIP AND MISSION
FOR EVERYDAY PEOPLE

BOB ROGNLIEN

A Jesus-Shaped Life
Discipleship and Mission for Everyday People
© Copyright 2016 by Bob Rognlien

Published by GX Books

Design: Blake Berg

ISBN: 978-0-9973058-0-7

DEDICATION

To my beloved Pamela, who has shared this global adventure of discipleship and mission with me for the past thirty years. Thank you for making me more like Jesus every day.

CONTENTS

introduction

WHAT IS THE SHAPE OF
YOUR LIFE?

1

The Shape of our Lives

WHAT KIND OF SHAPE ARE YOU IN?

As a freshman in college, I was in the best physical shape of my life. Because I was a member of the football team, I was running, lifting weights, and training five days a week with my team-mates. I was in peak physical condition as an 18-year-old, but there were other aspects of my life that needed a serious workout. Relationally, I tried to face the challenges of college largely on my own. Vocationally, I focused primarily on my own needs and interests to the exclusion of others. Spiritually, I believed in God but had not yet yielded to the implications of following Jesus. I was in great

physical condition, but looking back I can see now that I was not in great shape.

Whenever we watch television, read a magazine, or surf the internet, we're bombarded with explicit and subliminal messages about the shape our life should take. Impossibly proportioned models aided by plastic surgery and digital editing show us the physical ideals we are supposed to attain. Sensational accounts of lavish celebrity lifestyles describe the economic standards of happiness. Scintillating gossip blogs and scandal sites narrate the sexual and relational escapades that promise at least a fleeting shot at fulfillment. Characters in films and television shows become the artificial examples we aspire to emulate.

Subtle forces all around us shape the goals and direction of our lives, often without our realizing it. We are all molded by messages we have received that define "success." The treatment we receive from peers and role models tells us who we are and what we should be doing with our lives. Through it all, the American Dream pervades our values with its insistent message: study harder to get good grades that will get you into a prestigious school so you can land a decent job and earn a big income which will help you find an attractive spouse with whom you can by a big house and drive nice cars and raise successful children and on and on.

Sooner or later each of us have to come to the place where we challenge these forces that seek to conform us to their own image. We have to ask a deeper question:

What shape is my life meant to be?

This question must ultimately lead us beyond ourselves, and even the world we live in, to the one who designed us and called us into being. The Bible tells us that in the very beginning God created us in his image—which means our lives are designed to be shaped above all by a relationship with our Creator.

THE SHAPE OF A NEW KIND OF LIFE

Two thousand years ago a Jewish Rabbi from Nazareth entered the stage of history and invited ordinary people to follow the pattern of his life. He gave us a new basis for our identity by personally relating to God as his Daddy and teaching his followers to do the same.

Jesus told his closest friends, *"For I have given you an example, that you also should do just as I have done to you."* (John 13:15) He went on to say, *"Whoever has seen me has seen the Father."* (John 14:9) In so doing, Jesus explicitly claimed to be the living template for the life we are meant to live.

At first Jesus seemed like many teachers of his time, but soon it became clear that his was a life unlike any other. Jesus taught with unprecedented authority and healed with indisputable power. Jesus welcomed outcasts rejected by the religious establishment and declared their sins forgiven. He told people about a New Covenant that overcame the separation between God and his children. He cast a powerful vision of God's Kingdom—a world where God's will is done on earth as it is in heaven. Soon large crowds gathered to hear his message of Good News and began to experience the freeing power of that Kingdom as it flowed through him.

> Sooner or later each of us have to come to the place where we challenge these forces that seek to conform us to their own image. We have to ask a deeper question:
>
> What shape is my life meant to be?

From these crowds, Jesus gathered a smaller group of disciples and invited them to share every aspect of his life. They went where he went, ate where he ate, and slept where he slept. They lived in the kind of relationship with Jesus that taught them to know what he knew, and also to do what he did, so they could ultimately become like him. Before long he was training them to go out on their own to preach the Good News of the Kingdom, heal the sick, and cast out demons.

Rejected by his own extended family and the people of his hometown, Jesus gathered these twelve disciples, along with their families and close friends, to form a new kind of extended spiritual family. As they shared their lives together, this new family became the base for their mission. They met in the courtyard and rooms of a large home, and Jesus showed his disciples how to disciple others and minister to those who were broken. Jesus explicitly trained seventy-two of these extended family members to take the Good News to people who had not yet experienced its transforming power. He taught them how to share God's peace with strangers and invest in those who were responsive. He gave them his authority and power to do the very same things they had seen him do.

The temporal and religious authorities soon recognized the threat posed by this multiplication of authority and power. They moved quickly to protect their own status and attempted to squash this movement by cutting off its head. Their plan to brutally execute Jesus on a Roman cross should have neutralized his followers through intimidation and a leadership vacuum, but it had the opposite effect. When his followers saw the crucified Jesus unmistakably alive again, they experienced a life-giving power that sustained them through the untold trials to come. In Jesus' sacrificial death, they found the source of the forgiveness he had proclaimed. In Jesus' glorious resurrection, they found the fulfillment of his promise that they would live forever in his Kingdom.

Fifty days later the followers of Jesus were dramatically filled with the Holy Spirit as Jesus promised. This experience of God's presence and power within them produced a quantum leap in their ability to do the things Jesus modeled for them. Large crowds gathered in Jerusalem, attracted by the liberating power of God released through them. The movement Jesus began continued to grow through multiplication rather than addition, because its leaders followed Jesus' example of training smaller groups of disciples who could do what they did. The results were exponential. These rapidly multiplying disciples gathered by the housefuls in extended spiritual families, and this pattern of life provided the support they needed to continue expanding Jesus' mission in spite of great pressure against them.

Like the authorities in Jerusalem who tried to stamp out Jesus' movement at its inception, officials across the Roman Empire desperately tried to halt the movement's rapid expansion through increasingly brutal and public intimidation. But it was to no avail. Because the basic DNA of Jesus was being replicated in each disciple through the process of multiplication, there were always more followers ready to take the place of those who were executed or banished. Because they lived as part of an extended family that shared a common mission, they were able to continue carrying out their commission in the face of constant opposition. Because they claimed the authority Jesus had given them and yielded to a power greater than themselves, they were able to overcome otherwise impossible obstacles.

Over the next three centuries, in the face of increasing opposition, more and more lives were shaped by the life of Jesus. The growing movement literally changed the course of human history. Today over a billion people claim Jesus as Savior and look to his example and teaching to shape their lives.

WHAT WILL SHAPE YOUR LIFE?

Eventually we all have to come to terms with the forces that are shaping our lives. Years ago our neighbors were doing some landscaping and I noticed something strange had appeared in their front yard. It was a chicken-wire frame formed into the shape of a jumping dolphin. Beside it was a second, smaller wire-framed dolphin. As I came nearer I could see that they had planted two small shrubs which were poking up inside the wire forms. Then I understood what they were doing. Their plan was to water and fertilize the shrubs so they would grow up into the wire forms. As the branches of the shrubs started to poke out of the wire forms, they would prune the shrub until it took on the shape of the form.

A few days ago I went out to check on the progress of the shrubs and was pleased to see one of the shrubs had grown up to completely fill the wire form. However, closer inspection revealed that the smaller wire form was still empty, with just a single branch inside of it. The contrast was striking. One shrub had been transformed into a four-foot tall green, leafy dolphin leaping out of the grass in the middle of their front yard. The other shrub was just a bare stick enclosed by an empty wire form.

After warning them about false teaching and deceptive practices, the Apostle Paul told the Ephesians *"we are to grow up in every way into him who is the head, into Christ"* (Ephesians 4:15). Jesus is meant to be the form that shapes our lives. We are meant to grow up and be pruned back until we begin to look and act more like him. When Jesus said, *"Follow me,"* he was inviting us to become a dolphin rather than a stick! This book is an invitation for you to grow more intentionally into the shape of Jesus.

If you have not yet gotten to know Jesus personally, he is knocking on your door, asking to come into your life. All it takes to begin this most incredible journey is saying yes and welcoming him in. As Jesus' Word speaks faith to your heart and his Spirit begins to fill and guide you, your life will take on a new direction and character. This amazing process continues as you open yourself to others who are following Jesus and allow them to help you learn how to let Jesus shape your life into something wonderful.

If you do know Jesus and have put your faith in him, this book is an invitation to go farther. Jesus came not only to save us, but also to remake us in his own image so we might be part of his great plan to save the whole world. In these pages you will find biblical tools to live a more Jesus-shaped life of discipleship and mission by his authority and power. This is what God has done in my life and in the lives of those closest to me. This is what God is doing in the lives of thousands of people around the world

> This book is an invitation for you to grow more intentionally into the shape of Jesus.

who are part of a movement that this book represents. Our hope and prayer is that by learning to follow the Way of Jesus more closely with us, you will be empowered to help others live a more Jesus-shaped life as well.

REFLECT, DISCUSS, AND RESPOND

1. What are some of the forces that have shaped your life?

2. What aspects of Jesus' life do you admire?

3. What do you think God might be saying to you right now?

4. What do you think God might want you to do in response to what he is saying?

2

The Shape of Jesus' Life

HOW MANY DIMENSIONS IN YOUR WORLD?

Imagine life without dimension. It's hard, because we only know a dimensional world, but try for a moment. Remember your geometry class? Life without dimension means you can't move up or down. You can't move to the left or to the right. You can't go forward or backward. You can only be where you are. A non-dimensional world is literally a single point with no volume.

Now let's move into one dimension. You can't move up or down. You can't move to the left or to the right. You can only go forward or backward. Your world is an infinitely narrow line. Like the one-dimensional point, it has no width whatsoever—it is thinner than the thinnest thread. This thin line goes on forever in each direction.

When we add a second dimension, our line becomes a plane. In this two-dimensional world, you can move forward and backward. You can move to the left and to the right. In fact, you can move in every horizontal direction. But there is no moving up or down, not even a little bit. Again, this plane is immeasurably thin, like the thinnest sheet of paper. There is no vertical dimension. Those who inhabit a two-dimensional world can only see the edge of things. It is impossible to look down on anything, because there is no up or down.

If a three-dimensional object or being were to enter into a two-dimensional world, it would appear as a flat shape, because only a slice of its form would fit into this plane. For instance, a sphere would appear as a circle and a cube would appear as a square. Imagine how difficult it would be for the inhabitants of a two-dimensional world to comprehend a three-dimensional visitor. They would only see an infinitely thin slice of that visitor—and even that would be visible only from its razor edge.

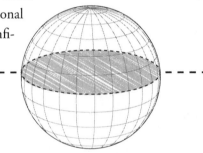

THE THREE DIMENSIONS OF JESUS' LIFE

When Jesus appeared in Galilee proclaiming the Good News of God's coming Kingdom, he was describing a new kind of reality. It was no less revolutionary than trying to describe a three-dimensional world to the inhabitants of a two-dimensional one. Knowing this new reality would be nearly impossible to understand and receive simply as an abstract concept, Jesus not only talked about it, but also demonstrated it through his own life and the impact he made on others. Ultimately Jesus made it possible for people not only to see this three-dimensional reality in his life, but to enter into that new reality themselves.

Jesus lived, and invites us to live, a three-dimensional kind of life. One day in the life of Jesus illustrates these three relational dimensions:

UP   with the Father

IN   with the disciples

OUT   with the world[1]

When Jesus decided to form his core group of disciples, he withdrew to a remote mountainside where *"all night he continued in prayer to God."* (Luke 6:12) This vividly describes the primary dimension of Jesus' life: his relationship with the Father. This dimension was so central and profound that Jesus described it this way, *"Truly, truly, I say to you, the Son can do nothing of his own accord, but only what he sees the Father doing. For whatever the Father does, that the Son does likewise. For the Father loves the Son and shows him all that he himself is doing."* (John 5:19-20)

After he spent that night in prayer, Jesus carefully chose twelve disciples in whom he would invest his life (Luke 6:13-16). Discipleship in first-century Palestine was a deeply committed covenantal relationship in which the rabbi invited his disciples to share every aspect of his life so they could become like him and do what he did. For the rest of his ministry on earth, Jesus lived in intentional community with these twelve disciples and a wider circle of disciples whom he called friends. Jesus could have decided to proclaim his message as a solitary sage and preacher, but instead he intentionally chose to live in close relational connection with others. This is the second key dimension of Jesus' life, modeled on the last night he was with his disciples. After washing their feet and sharing a sacred meal he said, *"A new command I give*

> Ultimately Jesus made it possible for people not only to see this three-dimensional reality in his life, but to enter into that new reality themselves.

you: Love one another. As I have loved you, so you must love one another. By this everyone will know that you are my disciples, if you love one another." (John 13:34-35)

After Jesus came down from the mountain with his twelve disciples, he joined with a larger group of his followers, while a crowd of people from all over Israel and the wider region of Palestine gathered around him as well. He proclaimed the Good News of the new Covenant God was making with his people, and the powerful Kingdom that was being unleashed. Jesus described this Covenant and Kingdom with words, and also demonstrated it by his actions. As Jesus claimed the authority given to him by the Father, divine power flowed through him to heal the broken and release those trapped in spiritual captivity (Luke 6:17-19). Jesus didn't limit himself to the two dimensions of a relationship with God and the supportive relationships of community. He also lived in this third dimension by reaching out with God's love and power to those in the wider world. As he put it when visiting the home of Zacchaeus the tax collector, *"For the Son of Man came to seek and to save the lost."* (Luke 19:10)

This powerful third relational dimension, flowing out of the depth of the other two, made Jesus' life truly revolutionary. The very idea of building relationships with such outsiders was controversial among the religious leaders of his day. When Jesus invited a hated tax collector named Levi into his closest circle of followers and had dinner at Levi's home with his extended family and friends, the Pharisees and teachers of the law complained to his disciples, *"Why do you eat and drink with tax collectors and sinners?"* Jesus responded by comparing himself with a doctor caring for the sick, explaining that his calling was the transformation of broken lives (Luke 5:30-32). Jesus' opponents vehemently tried to deny that the powerful impact he had on these outsiders was real, even seeking to discredit Jesus' power by calling it demonic (Luke 11:15). But the fruit of Jesus' life was undeniable. The power that flowed through him was obviously good and from God, because it consistently produced healing, wholeness, reconciliation, and liberation.

THREE DIMENSIONS IN OUR LIVES

In order to remember the pattern of Jesus' life and pass this on to others, we like to use the simple shape of a Triangle, each point representing one of these three dimensions:

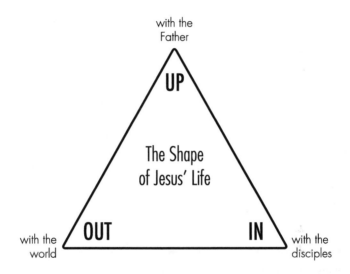

This picture of the three dimensions is a powerfully transferable tool that helps us follow Jesus and train other disciples to make disciples as well. The Triangle operates like a template, helping us gauge our growth as we become more like Jesus by growing in these three key aspects of our lives.

The first time I met people who were explicitly seeking to measure and balance their own lives based on the three dimensions of Jesus' life was when I was visiting a church in northern England that uses this tool. My friend Greg and I were staying with a lovely family from the church. About the second day we were with them, the husband Pete explained why he was going to visit the soup kitchen that Saturday morning: "I think my UP is pretty healthy and my IN is going well, but I sense God has been calling me to focus on my OUT lately. So I am going to see if this might be a place where I can grow in my care for those outside the church." At the time I still didn't fully understand the language he was using, but it was clear that Pete had a tool that was helping him learn how to allow the shape of Jesus' life to shape his life.

Since then God has used this biblically-based tool, and many others, to help me learn how to follow Jesus more closely and become more like him. The same is true for my wife, Pam, and the people closest to us. As we regularly reflect on the UP, the IN, and the OUT dimensions of our lives, the Holy Spirit has stretched and grown us in all three directions. This simple three-dimensional language now shapes the way we function in our marriage and family. It gives us a way to remember and talk about living lives shaped by Jesus' life.

Picture the impossibly cramped confines of living in a two-dimensional world, and then imagine the wonder of stepping into the expansive realm of a three-dimensional world. In Jesus' three-dimensional Kingdom, our capacity for living the life we were designed to live dramatically increases. That is what Jesus means when he says to those who will follow his voice, *"I came that they may have life and have it abundantly."* (John 10:10) This abundant life is not necessarily filled with more possessions or pleasures, as Jesus and his early followers demonstrate, but it is a life with greater capacity for what Jesus called *"complete joy"* (John 15:11). In this three-dimensional Kingdom, not only does our cup overflow, but the capacity of our cup increases.

In Jesus' three-dimensional Kingdom, our capacity for living the life we were designed to live dramatically increases.

REFLECT, DISCUSS, AND RESPOND

1.   How would you describe the shape of your life?

2.   In what ways is the shape of Jesus' life different from yours?

3. What do you think God might be saying to you right now?

4. What do you think God might want you to do in response to what he is saying?

3

The Shape of the Church

OUR EXPECTATIONS

When I pull into a gas station, I expect to be able to fill up my car efficiently, with as little distraction as possible. I park in front of the pump, swipe my debit card, open my tank, insert the nozzle, and begin pumping fuel. I don't really want anyone to talk to me, and I am not interested in shopping for anything else.

When my wife and I go to my favorite restaurant, I have different expectations. I expect to be warmly greeted and seated at a comfortable table, so I can enjoy delicious food. I want the server to be friendly and attentive without interfering in the conversation I am sharing with my wife or trying to become our friend.

When I go to the beach, I have yet another set of assumptions and expectations. The same is true when I go to my kid's school, attend a community play, or take a walk in our neighborhood park. We come to every experience with certain assumptions and expectations.

What are your assumptions about the Christian faith? What do you expect from a Christian church? Reflecting on your answers to these questions will help you understand and enter into the life we are meant to share together in community as the children of God.

Some people assume the church is meant to be an efficient vendor of religious services. They come once a week to fill up and don't really want anyone to talk to them or interact with them beyond what politeness requires. These people tend to see the pastor of the church as the religious provider who will explain the Bible to them and mediate regular access to God's forgiveness and guidance.

Others come assuming a full menu of spiritual options will be offered for their benefit. These people expect the church staff and dedicated volunteers to serve them and meet the needs and even whims of each family member. They understand the necessity to contribute financially in order to support the church staff that provides these services, and are willing to do so as long as their needs are met.

Some people come to church with anxiety and trepidation. Based on bad experiences from the past or negative portrayals they have received, these people assume they will find judgment, legalism, and prejudice when they come to church. They expect not to like church or its members when they show up, and sometimes they are right. Sometimes these are self-fulfilling prophecies.

Many of us bring other assumptions and expectations to church, such as the type of music that will be played, what will be included in the worship service, how the pastor will be dressed, how the building will look, what kind of terminology will be used, and much more. Ironically, though, not many of us assume we will encounter a community like the one Jesus built with his followers. Not many of us expect the people we meet at church will be like Jesus and do what he did. I say ironically, because being a Christian literally means seeking to be a "little Christ." Wouldn't it follow that the communities that bear Jesus' name would be patterned after Jesus himself? To put a finer point on it, why don't they? Let's take a closer look at the example Jesus set for us to follow.

JESUS AND THE SHAPE OF THE CHURCH TODAY

In Chapter One we began with a description of the movement Jesus initiated by multiplying disciples who could make disciples and teaching them to live in extended spiritual families that were on mission together. As they continued to do what Jesus did, thousands upon thousands found freedom from shame and healing from their brokenness through a Covenant relationship with Jesus and his family. They recognized their purpose in life was bigger than themselves or even their new spiritual families—that they were to be God's representatives bringing his transforming Kingdom to the whole world.

As housefuls of these disciples on mission formed across the Roman Empire, even the greatest temporal power in the world could not stop this movement of love and grace. Just as in the first spiritual family Jesus started back in Galilee, these churches welcomed ordinary men and women from the highest social strata of society, right down to the lowest of slaves and outcasts. As these missional families of Jesus' disciples shared the Good News of the Kingdom with power, lives continued to be transformed, and society itself began to change. Against all odds, even in the face of suffering and death, these new churches came to be known for the profound love they had for one another, just as Jesus had promised.

Looking at these historical facts reveals how the nature of the early church

Ironically, though, not many of us assume we will encounter a community like the one Jesus built with his followers. Not many of us expect the people we meet at church will be like Jesus and do what he did.

was qualitatively different than the church most of us know today. What happened to this contagious viral movement that overcame the oppressive powers of its day and altered the course of human history? Why are most churches in the western world shrinking in numbers and impact today? Why are so many people disconnected from the hope and power that Jesus offers? The answer is clear: somewhere along the way we lost a vital component of what Jesus started. The movement Jesus began has become for too many a religious institution rather than a dynamic way of life in a missional family.

After about three hundred years of learning how to do what Jesus did and empowering others to do the same, a critical shift took place in the Christian movement. Christians began to live their lives and form their communities after the pattern of the surrounding culture more than the example Jesus set. Increasingly the church and its leaders looked more like the institutions of the Roman Empire than the spiritual families of disciples Jesus sent out to the ends of the earth. Over the centuries that followed, the church continued to drift further and further away from the original shape of Jesus' life and the family he formed.

By the Middle Ages, church leaders had come to function as elite brokers of spiritual power, much like the feudal lords of European society. Church members were reduced to second-class citizens dependent on the spiritual patronage of the clergy, much like the serfs who worked their lords' estates. Periodically, new communities

of Christians emerged, calling the followers of Jesus back to their original pattern of life, but inevitably these movements slipped into their own forms of religious institutionalism. Still today we find that cultural influences, such as consumerism or inherited traditions, shape the lives of our churches more than the pattern set by Jesus.

But God seems to be doing something new in his Church today. Communities of Christians around the world are seeking to recapture the transforming power and purpose of those first three hundred years by learning from the example and teaching of Jesus and his first disciples. These churches, young and old, from nearly every tradition and background, have decided to build their lives together on the pattern of Jesus' life and the lives of those who followed him, rather than on inherited religious assumptions or current cultural trends. These churches want to grow communities of people who are becoming like Jesus and are learning to do what he did by living as spiritual families the way Jesus lived with his followers.

This means going back to the Bible and listening to what God tells us about who we are and why we are here. This means looking more carefully at the life of Jesus and learning how to allow his example to shape our lives today. This means understanding the way Jesus built community and building our lives together in the same way as those earliest Christians did. All of this begins by first considering the shape of Jesus' church.

THE SHAPE OF JESUS' CHURCH

One of the amazing things about Jesus is how he was able to train and empower others to do the very same things he did. What grew out of Jesus' three-dimensional life was both a group of twelve people living this kind of abundant, fruitful life, and also a growing movement made up of communities of people living as Jesus did, each one passing this way of life on to others. What made the first three hundred years of Jesus' movement so revolutionary, in contrast to the centuries that followed, is that the three dimensions of Jesus' life shaped not only individual lives, but the life of the Christian community itself.

Wouldn't you like to be a member of Jesus' church? Literally. Locally. What would your local church look like if Jesus was your pastor? To answer this question, we should look no further than the kinds of community Jesus formed. Not surprisingly, Jesus formed community in three dimensions:

UP   with the Father

IN   with the disciples

OUT   with the world

Jesus gathered with **large crowds** of people: *"a large crowd was gathering and people were coming to Jesus from town after town ..."* (Luke 8:4). When Jesus gathered large crowds together, he modeled all three dimensions of Kingdom life, but the dimension that people experienced most powerfully was the UP dimension. They heard God's authority in the teaching of Jesus. Together, they experienced God's power being released through his miraculous healings and his deliverance of people from demonic possession.

These churches, young and old, from nearly every tradition and background, have decided to build their lives together on the pattern of Jesus' life and the lives of those who followed him, rather than on inherited religious assumptions or current cultural trends.

Jesus gathered with a **small group** of disciples: *"And when day came, he called his disciples and chose from them twelve ..."* (Luke 6:13). When Jesus gathered a smaller group of twelve disciples together, again all three dimensions were functioning, but the IN dimension was most significant. They shared their lives together and built the closest kind of relationships with each other. Out of this deep connection and trust, Jesus was able to offer them the significant challenges that would form them into disciples who could do what he did.

Jesus gathered with **housefuls** of people: *"And when he returned to Capernaum after some days, it was reported that he was at home. And many were gathered together, so that there was no more room, not even at the door"* (Mark 2:1-2). When Jesus gathered with his followers at home, it was as an extended family of disciples on mission together.

> What would your local church look like if Jesus was your pastor?

They welcomed the outcast, the broken, and even the demon-possessed. They went out with Jesus on mission to seek and save the lost. This family was a small enough group to feel a strong sense of ownership for the mission he was entrusting to them, but large enough to provide a sense of strength and support to go out and face this huge challenge.

Looking carefully at the way Jesus built community, we can see that, while all of these expressions of community include the three dimensions of his life, each one was calibrated to help us become more like Jesus through each separate dimension.

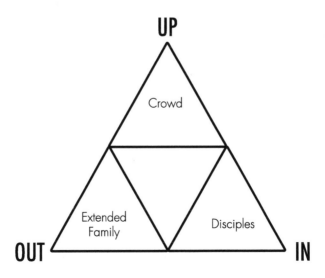

THE SHAPE OF OUR CHURCHES

For years the churches I led tried to attract new people through our many different staff-led programs, hoping this would produce disciples of Jesus who would carry out his mission. Ultimately, however, this produced more of a consumer culture than a discipling culture.

Now we realize it works the other way around. As we learn how to follow Jesus' three-dimensional example together and are empowered to live the kind of life he lived, we will naturally attract more people to join our family and empower them to join us in living out our destiny the way the first followers of Jesus did. We often assume that if we can build a great church, it will produce disciples. Jesus shows us the opposite is true. **If we learn to make disciples the way he did, it will produce a great church.**

When I first got a glimpse of a 21st century church that was shaped more like the first century church of Jesus, I found myself hungry to be part of that kind of community of missional disciples. The emphasis was not on getting people to attend the services and programs at their church facility, but on empowering people to represent Jesus in their everyday lives and share God's love in the real world. They did not trying to do these things by themselves, but as part of extended spiritual families that gathered in homes, parks, and pubs. Through intentional mentoring relationships, these people were learning to follow Jesus, share his love, and train others how to do it as well.

When I encountered this, I realized that if my own church was going to re-capture the discipling passion and missional power of the early church, we would need to learn how to live more like Jesus and form community the way he did. As Jesus said, *"I am the way, and the truth, and the life."* (John 14:6) Rather than basing the pattern of our life together on the way we had always done it in the past, or on the way our culture was telling us to live, we began to model our lives more intentionally on the actual way Jesus and his first followers lived. Not everyone in our church embraced this new direction, but those who did experienced significant change for the better and saw greater spiritual fruit in their lives and the life of their families.

Churches that are part of this discipling missional movement today have consciously decided to model their lives, individually and corporately, on the pattern Jesus set. Larger worship gatherings are designed to invite people into powerful experiences of the God who speaks and moves through his people today, calling for a response of faith. This is fertile ground for growth in the UP dimension. In these churches, smaller groups are not simply social gatherings to discuss biblical ideas, but are intentional discipleship groups (often called Huddles) where we speak God's Word into each other's lives as part of a discipling relationship. This is also where we offer supportive accountability to put into practice what we have heard. It's a powerful expressions of the IN dimension.

In addition to these familiar types of gatherings, churches have also begun to relearn how to build extended families on mission together. These Missional Communities are housefuls of people that offer both motivation and support to move out beyond the walls of the church, serve people where they are, and do with them the things Jesus did. It's a dynamic environment for expanding the OUT dimension.

These churches are intentionally formed around all three dimensions of Jesus' life, UP-IN-OUT, and seek to live out their mission together in the same expressions of community that Jesus and his first followers did.

In the next three parts of this book we will look more closely at the three key priorities of Jesus reflected in these three dimensions:

UP   Empowering people through God's
       Word of Covenant and Kingdom

IN   Developing a discipling culture that
       multiplies people who do what Jesus did

OUT   Releasing these disciples into missional
       families who are bringing God's
       Kingdom to the world.

Whatever your assumptions about Christianity or church, I invite you to set those aside and listen to what the Spirit of God is saying to you through the Bible, the pattern of Jesus' life, and the movement he began.

REFLECT, DISCUSS, AND RESPOND

1.   What are some of your assumptions about Christianity?

2.   What are some of your expectations of the church?

3.   Which one of Jesus' three key priorities do you need more in your life right now?

4.   What do you think God might be saying to you right now?

5.   What do you think God might want you to do in response to what he is saying?

part 1

WHAT IS MOST
IMPORTANT?

4

Who am I?

IDENTITY CRISIS

Not all questions are created equal. Some are trite and have little significance for our lives: How many angels can dance on the head of a pin? Others have huge implications: Will you marry me?

But two questions stand head and shoulders above the rest in terms of importance:

WHO am I?

WHY am I here?

These are foundational questions of being and doing, the question of our identity and our purpose. Answering them accurately is the key to the sense of satisfaction we all seek in life—the so-called pursuit of happiness.

But often we pursue what we think is happiness, only to discover it was all an illusion. When the dust settles and we reflect on our lives, we find ourselves still asking these same two questions. Thankfully, the Bible was written primarily to reveal the absolutely true answers to these two most important questions.

When Pam was pregnant with our first child, she knew well ahead of time that, if it was a boy, she wanted to name the baby after my father: Robert Phillip Rognlien, III. Two and a half years later, when she gave birth to our second son, we hadn't yet settled on a name for the child. I remember going home from the hospital that night marveling at my newborn son, but feeling surprisingly uneasy because we hadn't yet named him. It seemed in some intangible way like he was vulnerable without a name, as if his identity were somehow in question. I was very relieved the next day when we settled on a suitable title for him: Luke James Cady Rognlien.

The naming of a baby is symbolic of our basic human need to establish a sense of identity. A person's name the first thing we generally ask about when we meet him or her, because we are looking for a way to identify who this person is. Then we generally ask questions like: What do you do for a living? Where do you live? Are you married? Do you have kids? Having answers we feel good about to these basic questions is how we normally try to establish our identity.

We work harder in our job to achieve a title that will make us feel more important. We want to buy a home, drive a car, wear clothes, and obtain the possessions that will communicate success. We seek a spouse we can be proud of and who will reflect well on us. We hope our children will excel so they can achieve these same things, so we can be proud of them as well. The problem is that no matter how well we succeed at accomplishing these things, the answers we give to the questions above still feel incomplete until we address a deeper issue.

> These are foundational questions of being and doing, the question of our identity and our purpose. Answering them accurately is the key to the sense of satisfaction we all seek in life—the so-called pursuit of happiness.

WHO'S YOUR DADDY?

The Bible begins by clearly establishing our true identity—because the only one who can tell you who you really are is the one who made you. In Genesis 2 we read that God formed a man out of the dust of the earth and then formed a woman from the man. He breathed life into them and placed them in the Garden of Eden. Genesis 1 describes the nature of the relationship between Creator and his new creatures this way: *"So God created man in his own image, in the image of God he created him; male and female he created them."* (Genesis 1:27)

Being created in the image of God means that the Potter has left the imprint of his hand in the clay of our being. This imprint establishes God's primary relationship with us, since only his hand can adequately fill that void. We are created to be filled with the presence of our Creator, and nothing else will do!

This relationship between Creator and creature established our true identity in the beginning. The problem is that Adam and Eve didn't accept their

> Being created in the image of God means that the Potter has left the imprint of his hand in the clay of our being. This imprint establishes God's primary relationship with us, since only his hand can adequately fill that void.

identity, rebelling against God and deciding they could take his place. The relationship was broken, and we have been searching for our true identity ever since.

However, God didn't give up on man and woman, the pinnacle of his creation. Instead, he began the long journey of inviting them back into their defining relationship with him. In Genesis 3:21 we see how God made garments out of animal skins to cover Adam and Eve's shame. This is the first sign of what the Bible refers to as **Covenant**.

A covenant is an agreement that establishes a relationship between two parties. In covenant we say, "Who I am, and what I have, I give to you." Our covenant partner reciprocates with these same promises. Marriage is one of the few explicitly covenantal relationships that survive in our modern society.

Throughout the Old Testament, God makes a series of covenants with his people, each intended to restore us to our true identity through relationship with him. These biblical covenants, made through people like Abraham and Sarah, Moses, and David, were confirmed with various signs often involving the shedding of blood. Every day the priests offered animal sacrifices in the Temple in Jerusalem as way of participating in the covenant God made with his people.

The problem was that these Old Testament covenants fell short of reestablishing the original identity-producing relationship God had with Adam and Eve in the Garden of Eden. Finally, God spoke through the prophet Jeremiah, *"Behold, the days are coming, declares the LORD, when I will make a new covenant with the house of Israel and the house of Judah, not like the covenant that I made with their fathers on the day when I took them by the hand to bring them out of the land of Egypt, my covenant that they broke, though I was their husband, declares the LORD… I will put my law within them, and I will write it on their hearts. And I will be their God, and they shall be my people. And no longer shall each one teach his neighbor and each his brother, saying, 'Know the LORD,' for they shall all know me, from the least of them to the greatest, declares the LORD. For I will forgive their iniquity and I will remember their sin no more."* (Jeremiah 31:31-34)

Jesus fulfilled this incredible promise by establishing the long-awaited New Covenant through his own blood when he died on the cross and rose from the dead. This Covenant is mediated by Jesus himself, not priests carrying out sacrifices in a temple or services in a church. It is a Covenant of boundless grace in which God freely wipes away the sin and shame that has cut us off from our true identity. This is accomplished through the once-and-for-all sacrifice Jesus made for us on the cross.

We can only receive this gift of love and forgiveness in one way: by faith. When we put our faith in Jesus, receive the Holy Spirit, and trust God to resume his rightful place as the Lord of our life, we enter into the New Covenant which offers us the assurance of salvation and the restoration of our true identity as the children of God.

Jesus modeled this restored identity for us when he addressed God the Father as his Abba, or Daddy (Mark 14:36). He invited us to follow his example to claim our true identity when he taught us to pray, *"Our Father in heaven"* (Matthew 6:9).

The Apostle Paul discovered the joy and freedom of his restored identity by entering into this faith-based Covenant with Jesus and receiving the Holy Spirit. He explained it this way, *"For you did not receive the spirit of slavery to fall back into fear, but you have received the spirit of adoption as sons, by whom we cry "Abba! Father!" The Spirit himself bears witness with our spirit that we are children of God."* (Romans 8:15-16)

We can picture the New Covenant relationship this way:[2]

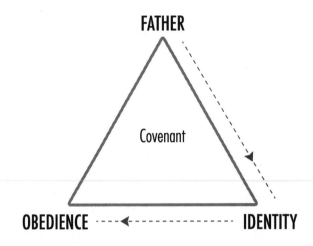

In Covenant we come to know God as our heavenly Father through the grace and love revealed in Jesus. This reveals our true identity. As we come to trust that God really is our Abba, and believe we really are his beloved daughters and sons, our desire to do God's will begins to grow. In a Covenant relationship, obedience is not a heavy burden of obligation, but a light yoke joyfully accepted. John describes the implications of Covenant this way: *"See what kind of love the Father has given to us, that we should be called children of God; And so we are. The reason why the world does not know us is that it did not know him. Beloved, we are God's children now, and what we will be has not yet appeared; but we know that when he appears we shall be like him, because we shall see him as he is. And everyone who thus hopes in him purifies himself as he is pure."* (1 John 3:1-3)

One of the potential pitfalls of seeking identity from the Father is the assumption that we can establish our identity through obedience. Sincere believers throughout the ages have tried to find their identity and worth in God's sight by trying to please and obey him. Whether it was a Pharisee named Saul of Tarsus zealously guarding the Law by persecuting the first followers of Jesus, or an Augustinian monk named Martin Luther flagellating himself in a German monastery, the result is always the same—legalistic religion. These saints who have gone before us have conclusively demonstrated it is impossible to obey our way to the Father.

Faith in the grace of Jesus is the only way our identity can be restored and genuine obedience can begin. Paul explains, *"For by grace you have been saved through faith. And this is not your own doing; it is the gift of God, not a result of works, so that no one may boast. For we are his workmanship, created in Christ Jesus for good works, which God prepared beforehand, that we should walk in them."* (Ephesians 2:8-10)

We can picture these two differing paths to identity and obedience this way:

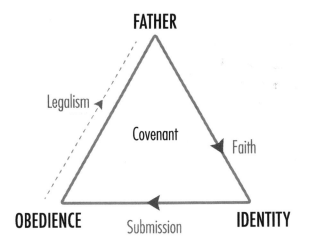

Legalism is always a dead-end street. It falls short of establishing our true identity every time. The grace and mercy of the New Covenant which Jesus made possible through his death and resurrection is the only way for us to discover who we really are. By faith in Jesus we are adopted as God's daughters and sons for all eternity. As we receive him and give him more control of our lives, the indwelling Holy Spirit naturally produces the desire to do his will on earth as it is in heaven. As we submit to him, we begin to learn how to do his will—how to obey.

When we put our faith in Jesus, receive the Holy Spirit, and trust God to resume his rightful place as the Lord of our life, we enter into the New Covenant which offers us the assurance of salvation and the restoration of our true identity as the children of God.

In this Covenant of grace, God is offering to adopt you as his own daughter or son. You are his child, and the Holy Spirit is calling you to live the life you were meant to live in relationship to your heavenly Father. In this relationship you have been promised an inheritance—the coming Kingdom of God.

Here lies the one true answer to the age-old question, "Who am I?" The truest thing that can be said about you is that you are a precious and loved child of God, his own daughter or son. Receiving God's freely-given grace by faith in Jesus means your true identity is fully restored. You can enter into this most amazing covenantal relationship right now, simply by asking Jesus to forgive you, fill you with his Spirit, and take control of your life.

REFLECT, DISCUSS, AND RESPOND

1. In what ways have you tried to establish your sense of identity in the past?

2. How does it affect you to know that you are offered adoption as a child of God through Jesus' New Covenant of grace?

3. What do you think God might be saying to you right now?

4. What do you think God might want you to do in response to what he is saying?

5

Why am I Here?

SEARCHING FOR PURPOSE

I had lots of dreams when I was a boy. I dreamed of being an explorer like David Livingstone and discovering exotic new lands. I dreamed of being an oceanic researcher like Jacques Cousteau and living on a dive ship with submarines and scuba gear. I dreamed of being an architect who would build a stone and steel fortress dug into a mountaintop, where I would live with my glamorous wife like some kind of James Bond nemesis. But

our dreams have a way of fading away as we awaken to the harsh realities of life in the real world, don't they?

When we finish school and begin to try to make it in this harsh world, our dreams begin to seem foolish and pointless. We realize we need to support ourselves and those who now depend on us. We need a reliable spouse with whom we can raise our children. We need to be practical, and so we grudgingly settle for less than our dreams. Many people end up feeling trapped in a dead-end job by bills, a mortgage, and family responsibilities. Some resign themselves to a life of drudgery and live for the weekends. Others jump from job to job, trying to find a sense of purpose in their work. Still others pour themselves into their children, hoping to find meaning through them. Even those who are blessed with families they love, and work they believe in eventually end up sensing there must be something more.

Our childhood dreams and adult longings are instinctive expressions of the sense we innately have that our lives are meant for something greater than ourselves. In a self-centered, materialistic world, this instinct usually gets channeled into grandiose ideas with ourselves at the center. But eventually we come to realize this, too, is a dead-end street. Deep down in our hearts and souls, we long to live a life of significance and meaning. We want to matter, and sooner or later it leads us to ask, "Why am I here?" Unfortunately, most of us feel powerless to fulfill whatever answer we might find to this question.

THE COMING KINGDOM

The Bible is very clear: you were created for a reason. There is a greater purpose to your life. It has been so from the very beginning. Remember: Genesis 1 tells us that God created us *"in his image,"* meaning for relationship with him. The very next verse tells us the rest of the story: *"And God blessed them. And God said to them, 'Be fruitful and multiply and fill the earth and subdue it, and have dominion over the fish of the sea and over the birds of the heavens and over every living thing that moves on the earth."* (Genesis 1:28) Not only did God create us for relationship with him, but he also gave us the mandate to rule creation on his behalf. We were created to be

God's fruitful representatives, making sure his will is done on earth as it is in heaven. This is what the Bible refers to as God's **Kingdom**.

> Deep down in our hearts and souls, we long to live a life of significance and meaning. We want to matter, and sooner or later it leads us to ask, "Why am I here?"

Sadly, Adam and Eve forfeited this role when they decided to pursue their own will rather than their Creator's. But God refused to give up on them. They broke their relationship with him, but God invited them back into Covenant with him. In the same way, Adam and Eve forfeited their role as his representatives, but God also called them back into his Kingdom. When God established a Covenant relationship with Abraham and Sarah, he also gave them this promise of purpose: "in you all the families of the earth shall be blessed" (Genesis 12:3). Through this Covenant the people of Israel were called to model for the rest of the world our role of representing God and promoting the goodness and blessing of his reign on earth.

As with covenants in the Old Testament, this representation fell profoundly short. Through the prophet Jeremiah God promised a renewal of his purpose for us: *"For I know the plans I have for you, declares the LORD, plans for welfare and not for evil, to give you a future and a hope. Then you will call upon me and come and pray to me, and I will hear you. You will seek me and find me, when you seek me with all your heart."* (Jeremiah 29:11-13). God promises you a greater purpose, which alone will fulfill the longing in your heart and soul for significance. God goes on to say this purpose will grow out of a Covenant relationship; specifically, a relationship in which we seek him with all our heart.

Just as with the New Covenant, Jesus is the fulfillment of this promised restoration of purpose. When he began his ministry, Jesus announced, *"The time is fulfilled, and the kingdom of God is at hand; repent and believe in the gospel."* (Mark 1:15) The gospel, or good news, was that Jesus had come to establish a new Covenant relationship of grace with us through faith. Jesus described the implications of that Good News when he said, *"the kingdom of God is at hand."* The Kingdom of God is the greater purpose that we were created for. The Kingdom is what happens when God's will is done on earth as it is in heaven. Jesus described the Kingdom of God in his parables and teaching, and he demonstrated it every time he fed the hungry, welcomed the outcast, healed the broken, liberated the oppressed, and raised the dead.

Jesus modeled our Kingdom purpose to represent God by carrying out his will on earth. His call was simple and clear: *"Follow me"* (Mark 1:17). Our purpose is to represent God and rule on his behalf by following the example of Jesus. Sounds simple, but obviously it is incredibly difficult. How are we to do the kinds of things Jesus did?

This is where the rubber meets the road, and we discover that the biggest obstacle to fulfilling our purpose is not answering the question Why am I here?, but finding the power to actually carry out that purpose.

POWER AND PURPOSE

When the Apostle Paul received the grace of God in Jesus he discovered who he really was as a son of God. But that Covenant relationship led Paul into his Kingdom purpose to become the apostle to the Gentiles (Galatians 2:8). **Every** child of God is given a role in God's Kingdom. No one has to sit on the sidelines—we all get to play! Paul described it this way: *"But when the fullness of time had come, God sent forth his Son, born of woman, born under the law, to redeem those who were under the law, so that we might receive adoption as sons. And because you are sons, God has sent the Spirit of his Son into our hearts, crying, 'Abba! Father!' So you are no longer a slave, but a son, and if a son, then an heir through God."* (Galatians 4:4-7)

> Our purpose is to represent God and rule on his behalf by following the example of Jesus.

In this Covenant of grace, God has adopted you as his own daughter or son. As his child, you have been promised an inheritance. Our Covenant inheritance as daughters and sons of God is, of course, the Kingdom Jesus proclaimed so clearly. As Jesus promised, *"Seek his kingdom, and these things will be added to you. Fear not, little flock, for it is your Father's good pleasure to give you the kingdom."* (Luke 12:31-32) God is entrusting his Kingdom to those who are in Covenant with him. Covenant relationship is always meant to lead us into Kingdom representation. As we come to realize our Daddy is, in fact, the King of the universe, the implications of our identity become clearer.

In historical terms a kingdom is the territory where the king's authority is recognized and his power is effective. A kingdom is quite simply everywhere the king's will is enacted. Extending the reign of God on earth by representing him is our divine purpose. In the Covenant we discover God is our Father. In the Kingdom we discover our Daddy is the King of the universe. The sons and daughters of the King are given royal authority. This authority gives us access to the power required to carry out the King's orders.

We can picture our role in the Kingdom this way:

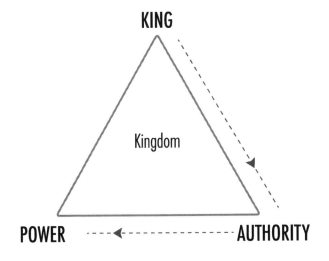

The reason Jesus was able to do God's will on earth as it is in heaven was that he claimed the authority given to him by his Father. From this authority flowed the divine power to feed the hungry, heal the sick, make the lame walk, and cause the blind to see. The only way we will ever fulfill our destiny is by learning from Jesus how to claim the authority he has given us. When we do, God's power will begin to flow through us—the power to represent him by carrying out his will.

It is critically important to remember the authority we are talking about is God's authority, entrusted to us by Jesus to do his will and not our own. If we are in Covenant with God through Jesus, we will seek his will above our own and operate in his authority, not our own. On the foundation of this kind of Covenant relationship, God can begin to build his Kingdom. Without that foundation we are simply building our own kingdoms, which are destined to crumble. Just as seeking our identity with the Father through our own obedience is a dead-end street, exercising spiritual power on the basis of our own authority is downright dangerous.

We can picture these two uses of authority and power this way:

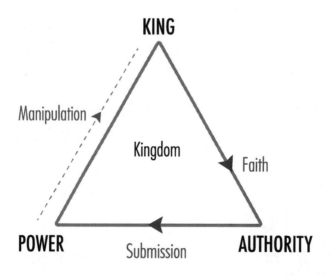

Faith is the way we claim the authority that has already been given to us. When we trust that Jesus really has given us all authority on heaven and earth and submit to God by acting on that authority, God's power starts to flow through us.

On the other hand, those who try to participate in God's reign by exercising spiritual power on their own authority inevitably end up manipulating others by imposing their own will under the guise of doing God's will. This quickly creates a coercive culture where spiritual abuse can abound. Rather than Spirit-led empowerment for the sake of others, this is a flesh-based exercise of power over others for selfish ends. One of the primary reasons some people see the exercise of spiritual power as intrinsically negative is because this is the kind of dynamic they have experienced or imagined. There is no room for manipulative power in Jesus' Kingdom.

> The only way we will ever fulfill our destiny is by learning from Jesus how to claim the authority he has given us. When we do, God's power will begin to flow through us—the power to represent him by carrying out his will.

You are a child of the King of Kings. He has given you the authority to act on his behalf, in his name. When you know who you are and who your Father is, you can claim the authority given you by faith and operate in his transforming power. By that power you will be able to obey him in ways you never could on your own. This is the key to fulfilling your purpose and answering the question Why am I here?

REFLECT, DISCUSS, AND RESPOND

1. What are some dreams you have given up on that might have come from God?

2. What are some ways you could begin to claim the authority given to you as a child of God so that you might be empowered to do his will?

3. What do you think God might be saying to you right now

4. What do you think God might want you to do in response to what he is saying?

6

The Power to Fulfill our Destiny

THE IMPORTANCE OF POWER

When I was a kid, my dad graciously allowed me to use any of the hand tools on his workbench. But the power tools were understandably forbidden. You can do a lot with a handsaw, hammer, and screwdriver, but there are obviously limits. Making flower boxes and birdhouses was cool, but I was drawn to the turned walnut candlesticks and the cherry colonial china cabinet my grandfather pro-  duced in his basement workshop. I ran my fingers over the curving surfaces of gleaming hardwood and marveled that he could craft such wonders.

I vividly remember the day my grandfather took me down into his basement and introduced me to the world of power tools. "This," he said, "is a table saw. You can do almost anything with it, and it can do almost anything to you." As carefully as a diamond-cutter taking hold of a raw stone, he took a chunk of oak, adjusted the rip fence, flipped the switch on the ancient saw, and firmly guided it through the blade, producing a perfectly straight and parallel cut in the hardwood. Wide-eyed with fear and wonder, I began to understand the potential of these powerful tools.

My grandpa went on to train me in the use of the joiner, the bandsaw, the drill press, the shaper, and (my favorite) the lathe. He would show me how to adjust each one's settings, how to operate its levers, and how to hold the wood. And then he flipped the switch. The machine began to whir, and sawdust started to fly. I loved the smell of hardwood blending with machine oil—it was an intoxicating blend that spoke of the creative masterpieces these tools could produce. And it all happened at the flip of a switch. If you cut off the electricity to that magical workshop, everything comes to a screeching halt. None of those tools can produce anything of value if they don't have enough power.

Of course, the same is true of the purpose God has called us to. It's fine to answer the question "Why am I here?" by saying we were created to carry out God's Kingdom. But unless we learn to operate in God's power, we will never be able to fulfill our destiny. Participating in God's Kingdom means representing God by doing his will on earth as it is in heaven, just as Jesus did. We may smile politely and nod in agreement with this in theory, but inside we know we will never do it, because obviously that is stuff that only Jesus has the power to do.

Or is it?

HOW DID JESUS DO IT?

Mark begins his account of Jesus' life by describing his baptism: the heavens were torn open, the Holy Spirit was poured out on Jesus, and his Heavenly Father spoke: *"You are my beloved Son; with you I am well pleased"* (Mark 1:11). It's hard to imagine a clearer or more convincing revelation of Jesus' true identity as Son of the Father.

After Jesus' baptism *"the Spirit immediately drove him out into the wilderness"* to face forty days of fasting, trials, and temptations (Mark 1:12-13). We can imagine this might not have been Jesus' first choice of post-baptismal activities, but he faithfully followed the Spirit's leading anyway. Jesus'  identity was connected to his obedience. When you come to know that you are a child of the Father, you desire to be faithful to your Father's will.

Ten verses later, when Jesus began teaching in the Capernaum synagogue, his listeners' various reactions point to the significance of Jesus' identity revealed in his baptism; "And they were astonished at his teaching, for he taught them as one who had authority, and not as the scribes." One of the reactions to his startling authority came from a demon-possessed man who cried out, *"What have you to do with us, Jesus of Nazareth? Have you come to destroy us? I know who you are—the Holy One of God!"* Jesus' response was simple and straightforward: *"Be silent, and come out of him!"*

It's fine to answer the question "Why am I here?" by saying we were created to carry out God's Kingdom. But unless we learn to operate in God's power, we will never be able to fulfill our destiny.

As soon as Jesus left the synagogue, he went to Peter's nearby home and proceeded to heal Peter's fevered mother-in-law. This display of power led to an entire evening of healing and deliverance. *"And he healed many who were sick with various diseases, and cast out many demons. And he would not permit the demons to speak, because they knew him."* (Mark 1:21-34) We can see the clear connection between Jesus' identity as Son of the Father, the authority given to him, and the power to do his Father's will.

Jesus knew who he was because the Father proclaimed it in his baptism. Jesus claimed the authority given to him by this birthright and stepped out in faithful obedience to his Father. This was the secret of his transforming power. He taught his disciples who they were and showed them how to claim the authority he was passing on to them. They followed his example, exercising this authority by stepping out in faithful obedience to Jesus' call, and they were empowered to do the very things Jesus did. And God's Kingdom continued to come just as Jesus had promised.

For most of my Christian life, I assumed Jesus could do things I could never hope to do because he was God incarnate and I (thankfully) am not. The only problem with my assumption is that Jesus assumes the opposite. He called people to follow him as his disciples, which meant he believed they could learn how to do what he did. In fact, Jesus sent out his followers with the instructions, *"And proclaim as you go, saying, 'The kingdom of heaven is at hand.' Heal the sick, raise the dead, cleanse the lepers, cast out demons."* (Matthew 10:7-8) I have a hunch the disciples were thinking what I used to think—that this would be impossible. In spite of any misgivings, they stepped out in faith, claiming the authority of Jesus and obeying his instructions. Upon their return they joyfully reported that it worked! They were able to do the very things that Jesus had modeled for them.

And so are we.

> Jesus knew who he was because the Father proclaimed it in his baptism. Jesus claimed the authority given to him by this birthright and stepped out in faithful obedience to his Father. This was the secret of his transforming power.

FROM IDENTITY TO EMPOWERMENT

Authority is intrinsically connected to power. In our communities
we entrust certain people with the
authority to enforce the laws that
protect our common good. To
symbolize that authority we issue
them a badge. To empower them to
enforce these laws, we issue them a
gun. Ideally, when someone is act-

ing contrary to the good of the community, the ones we have authorized
will confront them, first by showing their badge to clarify they are acting
on behalf of the community. Then they will show their gun to demonstrate
they actually have the power to enact the will of that community.

Although we are painfully aware of the frequency with which this public
trust is violated through the abuse of authority and power, it doesn't change
the fact that we need those who will faithfully exercise both with justice on
behalf of the common good. Jesus shows us the same is true in the spiritual
realm. When the Father proclaimed Jesus' identity, he gave him the badge.
When Jesus claimed that authority, he received the gun. That is why the
demons were so afraid of him—he carried both the Father's badge and gun.

Because we share his identity as sons and daughters of God, Jesus is able to
pass on to us the same kind of authority to function in God's power that he
received. We do these things in Jesus' name. Doing things in someone else's
name means you have been authorized by that person to act on their behalf.
Jesus said, *"Whatever you ask in my name, this I will do, that the Father may
be glorified in the Son. If you ask me anything in my name, I will do it."* (John
14:13-14) He is not suggesting that tacking the phrase "in Jesus' name" to
the end of our prayers will make us all powerful. Jesus is simply explaining
that, because of the Covenantal relationship with our heavenly Father that
he makes possible, we have been given the authority to act on his behalf—

in my name. Jesus is promising that when we claim that authority by faith, God will give us the power to carry out his will—I will do it.

Jesus' name was the badge given to his disciples to act on his behalf and do the things he modeled for them. When they stepped out in faith and began to proclaim the Kingdom, heal people, and cast out demons, they didn't try to do it in their own strength or wisdom. They did it by the authority Jesus had given them—in his name. The result was that the same divine power for good that flowed through Jesus flowed through them to give faith, heal, and liberate. Jesus gives that same badge and gun to anyone today who by faith will claim his name in Covenant love and submit to his Kingdom leading through the Holy Spirit.

We can picture the life Jesus lived and the life he calls us to imitate in this way:

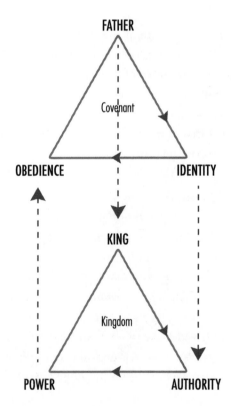

How did Jesus live the amazing life recorded in the Gospels? He did it by living simultaneously in both Covenant and Kingdom. In the gracious love of his heavenly Father, Jesus came to know himself to be the Son of God. (Father ➤ Identity) Realizing his Abba was the King of the universe (Father ➤ King), Jesus chose to claim by faith the divine authority that this identity carried with it. (Identity ➤ Authority) Submitting to his Father's will in Covenant faithfulness (Identity ➤ Obedience), Jesus exercised that authority so God's Kingdom power flowed through him. (Authority ➤ Power) This power served to accomplish the will of his Father and not just his own. (Power ➤ Obedience)

LEARNING TO EXERCISE AUTHORITY

As I learned more about my identity in Christ and how to exercise the authority he had given me, I began to experience God's power in new and wonderful ways in my life, my family, and our faith community. As our community grew in this, one of the things we noticed was a heightened sense of God speaking to us through Scripture, words, images, dreams and other experiences. As we studied more about prophecy in the New Testament, we began to learn how to intentionally listen to what God might be saying. As we grew in confidence, we learned how to speak those things into each other's lives to encourage and build one another up as Paul instructs in 1 Corinthians 14:29-33.

We were careful to temper this greater expression of spiritual authority with love and a low- control culture. Our language always reflects the fact that our perception of God's voice is fallible, and the recipient is free to take or leave what we think God might be saying to them. We have learned to say, "I think God might be saying…"

> Because we share his identity as sons and daughters of God, Jesus is able to pass on to us the same kind of authority to function in God's power that he received. We do these things in Jesus' name.

> As I learned more about my identity in Christ and how to exercise the authority he had given me, I began to experience God's power in new and wonderful ways in my life, my family, and our faith community.

rather than "Thus says the Lord!" We found this new experience of God speaking to us through one another exciting, faith-building, and incredibly helpful.

Another area where we learned to step into Jesus' power more consistently was physical healing. We had always prayed for the sick and injured to be healed, but now we had a growing sense of God's goodness toward us, our identity in Jesus, and the authority that gives us. We realized that praying in Jesus' name means exercising the authority he has given us to do the Father's will. We began to pray with greater confidence that a good Father always wants what is good for his children. As we exercised faith in the authority of Jesus, we prayed more boldly, declaring God's intention to heal and commanding anything standing in the way of that to leave.

The result of this newfound authority and boldness in prayer was that we started to see more dramatic physical healings than we had experienced before. A man's chronic back pain was instantly healed as we prayed for him at the end of a gathering in someone's home. A woman's bound shoulder was suddenly freed, and she recovered full range of motion while a group laid hands on her and prayed. A woman's cancer diagnosis was reversed overnight. A teenage girl was healed of her sprained ankle when the youth group persisted in prayer for her.

In addition to physical healing, more people began to share powerful experiences of emotional and relational healing as well. There started to be so many testimonies of healing in our community that I couldn't remember them all anymore. These experiences helped build our faith and confidence in exercising God's power in other areas of our lives.

As we learned how to exercise more of the authority Jesus has given us to do the will of our Father, we discovered it was not about esoteric techniques or attention-getting tactics. Jesus' healings and acts of deliverance were always characterized by a noticeable lack of complexity and showmanship. He simply commanded demons to leave, and they left. He declared people to be healed, and they were. Jesus was incredibly natural in the way he exercised supernatural power—he avoided the limelight. More often than not he told those he had healed to keep quiet about it!

We learned to step into God's power in the most normal way we could, so it would be clear any extraordinary outcome was God's doing and not due to our special technique or personal charisma. It has become increasingly natural for us to exercise God's supernatural power as he manifests himself in our lives. We are now in the habit of listening for God's voice and expecting him to reveal himself. We are used to sharing whatever we receive with others in the hope it will be helpful to them. As a normal way of life we pray with greater confidence and authority for God's Kingdom to break in and for the enemy to be thwarted. We are learning to live a naturally supernatural way of life as authorized representatives of our King.

Of course, not everyone we pray for is healed. We don't blame them for this, but simply recognize that as a community we have not yet grown in faith to place where we can win every battle. We do persist in seeking healing for those who continue to suffer, because this is what Jesus told us to do. There is a woman we see from time to time named Cindy, who was suffering from Lupus and Myasthenia Gravis, which caused her constant pain and significantly reduced her mobility. We prayed for Cindy to be healed, but her condition worsened. Before long she was struggling to walk with a cane, even though we persisted in prayer. Eventually Cindy was in even greater pain and confined to a wheelchair. We tried to exercise the authority of Jesus with all the faith and love we had, hoping something would change for her.

It was nearly two years later when we saw Cindy again. She was so dramatically improved we didn't even recognize her at first. When we realized who she was and asked her what had happened, she told us that during the final prayer session two years earlier she was miraculously healed! She stopped taking all her medications and her doctors told her the Lupus and Myasthenia Gravis was completely gone. Today there is no sign of her disease and she walks four miles in an hour every day!

As Cindy began to tell her story of healing that day, I felt a strange tingling in my lower back and radiating down my legs. For eight years I had suffered constant pain from two collapsed disks in my lower back. I had tried every imaginable treatment with no improvement and sought prayer for healing with no results. At first I thought the tingling was a spike of nerve pain that so regularly plagued me, but then I realized it felt good. Then I wondered if I was having an emotional reaction to Cindy's testimony, but it was much stronger than goosebumps. Finally I realized that I had no pain in my lower back for the first time in eight years! At first I was cautious to claim healing for fear the pain would return, but since that day I have had no pain to speak of in my lower back. Somehow just hearing Cindy's testimony finally broke through whatever was standing in the way of the healing I had sought for so long. Maybe it is what Paul wrote to the Romans long ago, *"So faith comes from hearing, and hearing through the word of Christ."* (Romans 10:17)

EVEN GREATER THINGS

On the last night he was with the disciples before going to the cross, Jesus explained the implications of finding our identity and authority in him: *"Do you not believe that I am in the Father and the Father is in me? The words that I say to you I do not speak on my own authority, but the Father who dwells in me does his works. Believe me that I am in the Father and the Father is in me, or else believe on account of the works themselves. Truly, truly I say to you, whoever believes in me will also do the works that I do; and greater works than these will he do, because I am going to the Father. Whatever you ask in my name, this I will do, that the Father may be glorified in the Son." (John 14:10-13)*

Notice the key points Jesus makes about the example he has set for us to follow:

1. Jesus lived in perfect Covenant union with the Father ("I am in the Father, and the Father is in me")

2. Jesus spoke on the basis of his Father's authority, not his own ("I do not speak on my own authority")

3. As a result, the Father's power flowed through Jesus ("but the Father who dwells in me does his works")

4. By faith we can do the same things Jesus did ("whoever believes in me will also do the works that I do")

5. As we yield control to the Holy Spirit, we can exceed Jesus' results ("and greater works than these will he do, because I am going to the Father")

6. Those who live this kind of life can literally do anything God calls them to do ("Whatever you ask in my name, this I will do, that the Father may be glorified in the Son")

Who am I? You are a child of God, adopted into his family by Jesus' Covenant of grace. Why am I here? You have been given authority to represent God and the power to carry out his Kingdom purpose on earth. The more deeply you trust the Father's adoption of you, the greater your desire to do his will becomes. The more fully you recognize your Father as the King of the universe, the greater your confidence in the authority he has entrusted to you becomes. The more you step out in faith by claiming that authority

> Who am I? You are a child of God, adopted into his family by Jesus' Covenant of grace. Why am I here? You have been given authority to represent God and the power to carry out his Kingdom purpose on earth.

and submitting to the will of your Father, the greater your ability to mediate God's transforming power to others becomes.

This is the secret to living the abundant, transformational, extraordinary life Jesus modeled for us. But it is not one we can live alone. In order to become who we are and fulfill our destiny, we need to learn how to develop Covenantal relationships and build Kingdom community.

REFLECT, DISCUSS, AND RESPOND

1. What is one way you could claim your Covenant identity more fully by faith so your desire to obey God would grow?

2. What is one way you could step into your Kingdom authority more fully by faith so God's power flowing through you would grow?

3. What do you think God might be saying to you right now?

4. What do you think God might want you to do in response to what he is saying?

part 2

WHO ARE YOU
FOLLOWING?

7

Follow Me

APPRENTICESHIP

I love to build things. It all started with Legos™. I spent untold hours creating outlandish spaceships or impossibly complex mansions—the kind I mentioned earlier where James Bond's nemesis plots world domination! As I got older, my building projects moved to the barn, since we didn't have a garage. I looked around at the scrap lumber and my dad's tool bench and tried to start to create a masterpiece. These masterpieces usually involved figuring out how to get a go-cart to roll faster down a hill or how to get a skateboard to fly higher off a ramp.

My construction urge did not grow in a vacuum. Since I can remember, I have watched my dad build things. When I was eight, we moved into a ranch house that the owner had not quite finished. I watched my dad hang drywall. I watched him cut moldings. I watched him hit his thumb with a hammer. Once the inside of the house was done, he moved outside. He built fences and gates. He built stalls in our barn. I was there on the sidelines, watching his every move.

As I got older, my dad started to involve me in what he was doing. I handed him tools. I held boards while he cut them. It wasn't long before he was showing me how to cut the boards and drill the holes. I got to be part of the process. Basically I imitated what I saw him do.

I mentioned earlier how my grandfather introduced me to power tools. One fall my grandpa came for a visit and brought his tools to help my dad with some projects on the house. Now I got to work with both of them. By listening, watching, helping, and participating, I gained more and more skills in carpentry and woodworking from these experienced mentors.

The culmination of this training came during my junior year in high school when I showed my dad the plans I had drawn for a large, three-level deck on the back of our house. He took one look and said, "Let's build it!" We spent that summer measuring, sawing, and hammering together. I went on to build custom homes through the summers of my college and graduate school years. During my last summer in construction, I was the foreman running the crew on a large home. By then I had learned pretty much every aspect of framing a house. I never attended a class on construction. I never read a book on carpentry. But I had skilled mentors who showed me how to do it, explained the finer points, invited me to try it out, corrected me when I made mistakes, encouraged my successes, and, when I was ready, set me out on my own to do what they did.

This is exactly how Jesus trained his disciples and taught them to train their disciples. For the first three hundred years this is how the movement of Jesus continued to spread like wildfire in spite of vicious persecution. This kind of mentorship is one of the things we have lost in western Christianity. Jesus is calling us to return to the pattern of discipleship he set for us.

FIRST-CENTURY RABBIS AND DISCIPLES

In first century Jewish society, the most important person in the community was the rabbi. He was the interpreter of the Bible, the leader of the synagogue, the arbiter of legal disputes, and the cornerstone of the educational system. When children were about five years old, they went to the synagogue to begin their basic education with the rabbis. Most students completed their education at the age of ten, but some went on to the next level of learning until they were about 15 years old.

At that point, a rabbi looked for those few exceptional students he believed had what it took to become talmidim, a Hebrew word we usually translate disciples. Talmidim came to live with the rabbi. They went everywhere the rabbi went, ate what the rabbi ate, and slept where the rabbi slept. They hung on his every word, watched his every step, and were ready to jump in whenever the rabbi asked them to join him in what he was doing. The point of discipleship in first century Judaism was to live in such a close relationship with the rabbi that, by following his example, you could learn to do what he did and so become like him. I love the ancient rabbinical blessing based on a passage from the Mishnah, "Follow your rabbi, drink in his words, and be covered by the dust of his feet."[3]

> The point of discipleship in first century Judaism was to live in such a close relationship with the rabbi that, by following his example, you could learn to do what he did and so become like him.

JESUS THE RABBI

When Jesus was walking along the shore of the Sea of Galilee and invited the fishermen busy at their work to "come follow me," he was inviting them to become talmidim. We expect them to answer, "Where are you going? How long will we be gone? What's in it for me?" Instead, "Immediately they left their nets and followed him "(Mark 1:18). Until we understand the nature of discipleship, we will be puzzled by this sudden and absolute response of the fishermen to Jesus' invitation.

To become a talmid was one of the highest honors someone could attain in first century Jewish society. It must have been shocking for these fishermen to receive this invitation from Jesus. After all, these were the students who did not make the grade. They left the synagogue school to learn a trade because they were not considered good enough to become disciples. Now this amazing Rabbi, Jesus of Nazareth, was inviting them to become his disciples—incredible! It would be like steel workers in Pennsylvania receiving a full scholarship from Harvard Law School and then being invited to become roommates with their favorite professor. No wonder they dropped their nets and followed Jesus!

Jesus eventually invited twelve very unlikely men to be his talmidim. Although they did not make the grade by the standards of their culture, in Jesus' eyes they had the potential to become like him and extend the kingdom he was inaugurating. For the next three years, Jesus invested in these disciples, sharing his whole life with them. During this time Jesus showed them how to live out God's Kingdom, invited them to participate with him, and then sent them out to do what he did on their own.

Jesus didn't send them out empty-handed. He gave them his authority so God's power could flow through them to carry out his will on earth as it is in heaven. Before his arrest and crucifixion, Jesus promised them, *"I will ask the Father, and he will give you another Helper to be with you forever, even the Spirit of truth... In that day you will know that I am in my Father, and you in me, and I in you... If anyone loves me, he will keep my word, and my Father will love him, and we will come to him and make our abode with him... the Helper, the Holy Spirit, whom the Father will send in my name, he will teach you all things and bring to your remembrance all that I have said to you."* (John 14:16-17, 20, 23, 26)

That promise was dramatically fulfilled on the day of Pentecost, and these disciples went out in the authority of Jesus and the power of the indwelling Spirit to do the things he had done, and then disciple others as they had been discipled by Jesus. This spark ignited a movement that literally changed the world. The Spirit is fanning that ember still, until it catches fire in those of us who claim to be the followers of Jesus today.

IN SEARCH OF A MENTOR

I have been a Christian for over 30 years now, but until eight years ago no one intentionally offered to disciple me. When I was in high school and came to faith in Christ, my pastor and youth director taught me about Jesus and the Bible, and I was influenced by their example. But they were not trained to disciple leaders, and so they did not intentionally build a discipling relationship with me. Over the years many other wonderful people in my life have inspired, encouraged, taught, and supported me, but no one ever invited me to follow them. No one

For the next three years, Jesus invested in these disciples, sharing his whole life with them. During this time Jesus showed them how to live out God's Kingdom, invited them to participate with him, and then sent them out to do what he did on their own.

ever asked me if I would like to build the kind of relationship with them that would help me learn through their example how to become more like Jesus and do the things he did.

When I heard people talk about discipleship, there was always a disconnect for me. I understood Jesus had disciples, and I had a vague sense that being a disciple of Jesus meant becoming more like him, but I had no clear sense of how that might happen. As a pastor I taught and preached on discipleship, but I assumed this was something you did on your own, because that's how I had to do it. I became a follower of Jesus by attending worship services, Bible studies, praying, and reading the Bible on my own. Eventually I joined small groups of people who were doing the same and started to get involved in leadership—mainly leading worship services, small groups, mission trips, and other church programs.

Whenever I heard someone use the word disciple as a verb, it always made me feel a little weird: "So and so is discipling me" or "I am discipling so and so." It sounded presumptuous and kind of cultish. Who are we to disciple anyone? Jesus is the one who makes disciples, not us—right? I suppose that, because nobody ever discipled me, I had a hard time imagining being disci-pled by anyone or having disciples who intentionally followed my example. But then the realization hit me that, if I was to become like Jesus and do the things he did, then I would necessarily have disciples like he did. I was not follow-ing Jesus' example and making disciples the way he made disciples. No one was doing this in my life either. This realiza-tion gave rise to a question—what does it actually mean to live as a disciple of Jesus and make disciples the way he did?

> In the last eight years, I have been profoundly impacted by ordinary people who have invested in me and invited me to learn by following their imperfect example as they follow Jesus. During that time I have had the privilege of doing the same in the lives of other people.

This began a journey of learning Jesus-shaped discipleship as a way of life. In the last eight years, I have been profoundly impacted by ordinary people who have invested in me and invited me to learn by following their imperfect example as they follow Jesus. During that time I have had the privilege of doing the same in the lives of other people. These discipling relationships are among the richest I have ever had, and they are producing more fruit for God's Kingdom than ever before. The same thing has happened in the lives of those who are closest to me and in the lives of those who have become spiritual family to us. Discipleship has become the fabric of our lives and the culture of our family. I can honestly say there is nothing more fruitful and fulfilling than learning how to be a disciple and make disciples the way Jesus did.

REFLECT, DISCUSS, AND RESPOND

1. Why is it significant that Jesus called people to be his disciples who society deemed unworthy?

2. In light of what discipleship actually means, how do you respond to Jesus' invitation to follow him?

3. What do you think God might be saying to you right now?

4. What do you think God might want you to do in response to what he is saying?

8

Repenting and Believing

JESUS' METHOD OF DISCIPLESHIP

If we want to become Jesus-shaped disciples who make disciples the way
he did, we need to consider his methodology. Jesus formed three types of
community: large groups, a mid-sized group, and a smaller group. It was in
the smaller group of twelve that he intentionally made disciples.

When Jesus called the twelve, he not only invited them to share life with
him, but also with each other. We often think of discipleship as a one-on-
one dynamic, but Jesus nearly always discipled people in the context of
community. Since Jesus did his primary discipling work in a small group of
twelve, we will also need to gather with others in smaller groups if we are
going to be discipled and learn how to make disciples the way he did. But
these are not the kind of small groups many of us are familiar with. These
groups include challenge and accountability.

Just before Jesus began calling disciples to follow him, he launched his ministry by describing the central dynamic of his discipling process: *"The time is fulfilled, and the kingdom of God is at hand; repent and believe in the gospel."* (Mark 1:15) The term translated time here is the Greek word kairos, which is quite different from the chronological passage of time. Kairos refers to a critical moment in time, a crossroads in which God opens up an opportunity to us and we are called to choose which way we will go. Jesus explained very simply how we become part of the Kingdom of God when we come to that crossroads:

Repent and believe.

The word repent is not so much feeling bad about things we have done wrong, as is often assumed. It literally means undergoing a change of mind and gaining a new perspective. When Jesus calls us to repent, he is inviting us to open ourselves to a new point of view, to God's point of view. Obviously, the only way to gain that point of view is to listen to what Jesus is saying to us. One of the easiest ways to answer this call to repentance is simply to ask yourself and discuss with others the crucial question:

Jesus, what are you saying to me?

This question might seem overly simple and obvious, but it is amazing how different your life becomes when you start genuinely wrestling with it on a regular basis.

We often think of discipleship as a one-on-one dynamic, but Jesus nearly always discipled people in the context of community.

This question is not meant to be answered alone, but with the direction of our rabbi and the input of our fellow disciples. As we allow the person discipling us to speak into our lives, along with those who are sharing this journey with us, we will begin to discern more clearly Jesus' voice speaking to us among all the other voices in our life. When he described himself as the good shepherd, Jesus explained that learning to recognize his voice is critical on this journey of discipleship: *And the sheep follow him, for they know his voice* (John 10:4).

But of course, hearing what Jesus is saying is only half the process. Even if we are able to identify the message Jesus has for us, that message necessarily calls for a response. That is why Jesus followed the call to repentance with a call to faith: *repent and believe*. The word *believe* is the verb form of the noun we usually translate *faith*. It means putting faith into action. The believe half of the equation is a call to trust Jesus enough to act on what he says to us, to follow where he is leading us. It is best expressed by the crucial second question:

> Jesus, what do you want me to do about what you are saying?

This is the question of response. It is not something we do out of a sense of obligation, but instead a step of faith empowered by the authority of Jesus and the presence of his Spirit within us. We ask the person discipling us and those in our group to help us formulate a concrete plan to put into action what Jesus is calling us to do. With a plan in place, the way forward now starts to become clearer.

There is a crucial third aspect of this process we might easily miss: accountability. The truth is, even if we hear what Jesus is saying to us and begin to understand what he wants us to do in response, a part of us will resist actually doing something about it. This part of us is what Paul refers to as the flesh rather than the Spirit in us. We need the support and encouragement of our rabbi and fellow disciples to help us overcome the pull of the flesh so we can yield to the power of the Spirit.

Once a plan starts to take shape, and we have identified the next step Jesus wants us to take, we agree on whom we will look to for supportive accountability. In our community, we express this follow-through with the simple question: How did it go? This is not an expression of judgment or pressure, but the loving follow-up of someone who cares enough to offer support because they want you to become more like Jesus and bear fruit for his Kingdom.

One important principle in this process that helps maintain a healthy balance is what we call Low Control/High Accountability. Low control means we do not have the right to tell anyone what they have to do. That would be manipulative and could lead to all kinds of destructive dynamics. Although we offer each other input and suggestions on what Jesus might be saying and what he might want someone to do, in the end that person alone has to decide what Jesus really wants them to do. Once someone has confirmed what they believe Jesus wants them to do, then it is up to the rabbi and rest of the group to offer the supportive, non-judgmental kind of accountability that help that person actually take a step of faith and move forward in God's Kingdom purpose.

We have adapted an incredibly helpful tool to help us remember the discipling method of Jesus and put it into practice—the Learning Circle[4]:

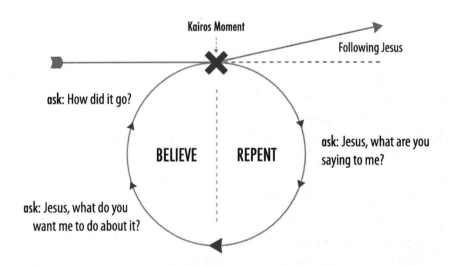

A *kairos* moment is an event, large or small, that begins the process by which Jesus wants to change our perspective and move us in a new direction. Repentance means we observe this event and begin to reflect on it by discussing it with others. Through this process we ask others to help us answer the question: Jesus, what are you saying to me? Believing means we respond by beginning to make a plan, establish accountability, and then step out in faith to follow the direction in which Jesus is leading us. Through this process we ask others to help us answer the question: Jesus, what do you want me to do about it? Those who agreed to offer accountability follow up by asking the question: How did it go?

This is the way Jesus discipled those who would go on to do what he did and change the world. This is how we are called to become like Jesus and help each other do the same.

LIVING IN A DISCIPLING CULTURE

For about three years, the twelve disciples of Jesus lived in a relationship with him that helped them learn what he knew, do what he did, and become like their Rabbi. After Jesus ascended into heaven, his followers continued to live in the kind of relationships that enabled them to do this with others. Their followers did the same. The followers of those people did it as well. This dynamic is what we call a **discipling culture**, and it is an incredibly helpful environment for anyone who wants to live as a fruitful follower of Jesus.

When Jesus interacted with his disciples, he regularly took them through the process of repenting and believing. Through this process he created what we call a High Invitation/High Challenge culture. High Invitation describes the willingness to live in a Covenantal friendship where there is a high level of investment and support being offered in return for the openness and willingness to receive it. High Challenge describes the willingness to speak words of truth into someone's life that call them to a life more fully reflecting God's Kingdom purpose. This is about living out the biblical DNA of Covenant and Kingdom with one another.

We can describe Jesus' discipling context this way[5]:

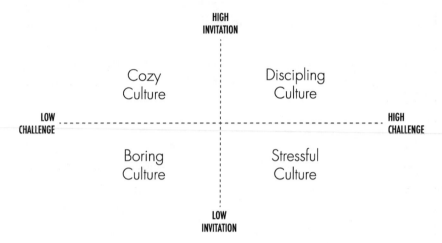

If no one is inviting you into supportive relationship, nor are they challenging you in any way, it creates a rather boring environment. The message is that no really cares enough about you to even notice. This is a Low Invitation/Low Challenge environment.

If someone offers you all the support you need, but never really challenges you, it creates a quite comfortable environment. This puts you in the role of a consumer. It is what we call a High Invitation/Low Challenge environment.

If someone presents you with a high level of challenge but does not offer a corresponding invitation to supportive relationship, it produces stress. Many people in the corporate world face this dynamic in their workplace. We call it a Low Invitation/High Challenge environment.

What Jesus offered is obviously described by the remaining quadrant, a High Invitation/High Challenge environment. He offered an incredibly high level of investment in people's lives, while at the same time calling them to ideals and purposes far beyond their own ability and strength. This combination is like mixing explosive chemicals—it makes a huge bang!

We all want to live a life of greater significance and meaning, but often don't know how to do it. We feel inadequate to face the task. But Jesus offered people both a life of eternal significance (Kingdom) and the relational resources that would empower them to live that life (Covenant). This is how he made disciples who could do what he did and who could go on to teach others to do the same.

As Jesus concluded his Galilean ministry and prepared to head toward his final destiny in Jerusalem, he took his disciples on a retreat to the far northern part of Israel, Caesarea Philippi. There he asked them, *"But who do you say that I am?' Simon Peter replied, 'You are the Christ, the Son of the living God.'"* (Matthew 16:15-16) Jesus responded to Simon's profession of faith with a huge Covenantal invitation. He gave him a new name, Peter, which literally means little rock. In the Old Testament God is repeatedly referred to using this metaphor: *"The LORD is my rock and my fortress and my deliverer, my God, my rock, in whom I take refuge, my shield and the horn of my salvation, my stronghold."* (Psalm 18:2)

Jesus gave Simon his own name, as clear an invitation to oneness in Covenant as when a bride and groom decide to share the same name. As if that weren't enough, Jesus then went on to entrust Peter with the metaphorical keys to his Kingdom. Jesus was telling Simon: everything I have, I give to you!

While Peter and the other disciples were still basking in the glow of this incredible invitation, Jesus then gave them the ulti-

> Jesus offered people both a life of eternal significance (Kingdom) and the relational resources that would empower them to live that life (Covenant). This is how he made disciples who could do what he did and who could go on to teach others to do the same.

mate challenge: *"If anyone would come after me, let him deny himself and take up his cross and follow me"* (Matthew 16:24). Now he asked them to give him their very lives in return.

Jesus used this careful calibration of Covenantal invitation and Kingdom challenge to create an energizing environment that drew people to give up everything to follow him. It was the kind of environment where his followers did far more than learn to recite theological ideas, follow religious rituals, or even observe ethical principles. It was the kind of environment that transformed simple, ordinary people into the kind of person Jesus was, the kind of people who could change the world!

REFLECT, DISCUSS, AND RESPOND

1. How would it affect you to have a spiritual mentor who regularly helped you answer the questions, "God, what are you saying to me, and what do you want me to do about it?"

2. What kind of invitation/support would help you become more like Jesus? What kind of challenge would help you become more like Jesus?

3. What do you think God might be saying to you right now?

4. What do you think God might want you to do in response to what he is saying?

9

Who are
Your Disciples?

RETURN ON INVESTMENT

Imagine a conversation with your stock broker that goes something like this:

> Hi Bill, how are you doing?
>
> Great Jill! How are things with you?
>
> Super. I was just calling to let you know about a new investment opportunity.
>
> I'm all ears. I have a bunch of cash sitting around that I really want to put into something worthwhile.
>
> Sounds like this is just the thing for you.
>
> How does it work?

You send in a deposit of $2,000 each week and I will transfer it to the fund.

OK. What then?

Well, the cash you deposit will accumulate in the fund at the rate of your deposits.

Hmm. What kind of return will I be getting?

Return?

Yeah, you know, like interest. Profit. Return!

Oh, that.

Yeah, that.

Well, this isn't that kind of fund.

Not that kind of fund?

No, this is more of a deposit kind of fund.

What does that mean?

It means you deposit the cash and we transfer it to the fund.

And nothing happens?

No, it just sits there.

What's the point of that?

Well, it gives you a place to deposit your money.

I'm sorry, but I thought you said this is an investment.

It is!

Well, I expect a return on my investment.

Oh. I guess this is not the fund for you.

Obviously not. Goodbye!

Bye.

Ridiculous, I know. No stockbroker would ever dream of trying to sell a fund that offered no return on the investment. If she did, no buyer in his right mind would put his valuable capital in such a fund.

Why do we assume Jesus would invest without return? Most Christians have a consumer mentality, and so we assume Jesus will give us things like grace, wisdom, and direction, while we will simply receive and enjoy these benefits with grateful hearts. Many of us assume Jesus does not expect anything specific from us. Of course, when we actually read the New Testament, we see nothing could be further from the truth.

Jesus told a parable meant to serve as a wakeup call for consumers: *"For it will be like a man going on a journey, who called his servants and entrusted to them his property"* The man gives varying amounts of money to his servants, and when he returns he calls them to account for what they have done with his resources. The ones who put the money to work and produced a return on his investment received a commendation: *"Well done, good and faithful servant! You have been faithful over a little; I will set you over much. Enter into the joy of your master."* The one who did not invest the money to produce a return got a very different response: *"You wicked and slothful servant!"* This unfortunate hoarder had his money taken away and was thrown into the outer darkness. (Matthew 25:14-30)

Jesus called disciples to follow him. He invested everything he had in them. After laying down his life on the cross and claiming the ultimate victory of resurrection, Jesus left those disciples with now-familiar marching orders: *"All authority in heaven and on earth has been given to me. Go therefore and make disciples of all nations, baptizing them in the name of the Father and of the Son and of the Holy Spirit, teaching them to observe all that I have commanded you. And behold, I am with you always, to the end of the age."* (Matthew 28:18-20)

> Many of us assume Jesus does not expect anything specific from us. Of course, when we actually read the New Testament, we see nothing could be further from the truth.

Jesus told his disciples it is now time for his investment in them to start producing a return. It is time for them to start doing the things he has done and passing that on to others to do the same. Jesus is not expecting them to do it on their own. He offers them all the authority on heaven and earth. The Father gave it to him, and it is now available to them because he is in Covenant with them. He gives his own name and that of the Father and the Holy Spirit. His promise is to be with them to empower their response.

Are you a disciple of Jesus? If so, are you also making disciples? Are you doing it the way Jesus did? I remember the first time someone asked me who my disciples were. It sounded so wrong. I shouldn't have disciples! Jesus is the one who has disciples. Yet Jesus says it as clearly as it can be said: make disciples.

This is our mandate. Paul understood this and was not afraid to call people to be his disciples. He repeatedly said things like, *"Be imitators of me, as I am of Christ"* (1 Corinthians 11:1). He made disciples who in turn could also make disciples. When he challenged the Corinthians to follow his example,

> Are you a disciple of Jesus? If so, are you also making disciples? Are you doing it the way Jesus did?

he pointed them to Timothy, whom he had discipled: *"I urge you, then, be imitators of me. That is why I sent you Timothy, my beloved and faithful child in the Lord, to remind you of my ways in Christ."* (1 Corinthians 4:16-17).

Jesus expected a return on the investment he made in his disciples. The return he expected was that they would make disciples, as he had done with them. Those disciples likewise were expected to bring the same return on the investment. This is how the Kingdom of God grows, by multiplication. This is how the early church was able to overcome the powers of Rome that sought to crush the movement Jesus started. No matter how many Christians the Romans executed, there were more disciples who were making disciples, so it grew exponentially. Nothing on earth could stop it! The same will be true today if we are willing not only to be discipled, but to start discipling others.

FORMING AN ENVIRONMENT FOR DISCIPLESHIP

If we are going to become disciples of Jesus and learn how to make disciples the way he did, we will need to be intentional about forming environments where this is possible. We need a place where someone can help us identify our kairos moments so we can begin to discern what Jesus is saying to us. This needs to be in the context of a small group of disciples who are learning this process with us. Their input will help us discern how Jesus wants us to respond in steps of faith. This needs to be a group of people who are not trying to manipulate or control us, but who love us enough to offer the accountability we need to actually follow through on what Jesus is calling us to do. In short, we need a group to help us repent and believe—a group like the one Jesus formed with his disciples.

We have come to call this kind of a discipling group a Huddle. As a football player, I always appreciated the importance of the huddle. Eleven guys come together to catch their breath, hear from their leader, and consider what it means for each of them. Then they go out together and put the plan into action to win the game. That's what Jesus did with his closest disciples.

A Huddle is a discipling group designed for those who have committed to leading others. You can also form small discipling groups for those who want to learn how to follow Jesus but aren't yet ready to commit to leading others. The process is the same in both kinds of groups. We use the simple Learning Circle tool to help us remember how to repent and believe as Jesus taught us. We repent by helping each other discern what Jesus is saying to us in our current kairos moment. We believe by committing to the step of faith we have identified Jesus is calling us to take. We receive as well as offer to others accountability that gives us the courage to actually follow through.

I'll never forget the first time I was in this kind of Huddle. I had participated in and led many small groups over the years, but this was different. We weren't just discussing hypothetical ideas—we were making it personal to our lives. We weren't just sharing our own opinions or advice—we were seeking to hear what God was actually saying in that moment. We weren't just encouraging each other—there was also an appropriate level of challenge that caused me to dig deeper and take an honest look at myself. I found myself excited by what God was saying to me and energized by the plans that came out of our discussion. After the Huddle I was excited to follow through on what we had talked about and took some significant steps of faith. I remember thinking, "If this is what Jesus-shaped discipleship is like, I'm in!"

In the years since, I have experienced God changing my life in so many ways through the process of repenting and believing in a small group Huddle. I never felt manipulated or coerced into something I wasn't ready and willing to do, but I have experienced great love, unconditional acceptance, and invigorating challenge. Through this process God has healed deep hurts, helped me overcome insurmountable obstacles, and empowered me to step into the things I knew he was calling me to do. I have grown in my ability to exercise Jesus' authority and power on behalf of others. As I have learned how to invite others into discipling relationships where we gather regularly in Huddle, my own fruitfulness has grown exponentially.

I encourage you to participate in this kind of a discipling community when you have the opportunity. As your fruitfulness grows, you will discover one type of fruit you were designed to produce is more disciples. This is the return on investment Jesus is looking for in you. For that reason, eventually you will be invited and challenged to begin the process of forming your own Huddle or discipling group. This is not something you are left to do on your own. The person discipling you will offer all the support and input you need so this challenge will be energizing and not overwhelming.

FINDING DISCIPLES

When Jesus invited people to come and follow him, they seemed to drop everything and come. Jesus lived a life others wanted to be a part of. He enjoyed parties. He ate and drank good food. He made friends with all kinds of people. He was a man of integrity who lived what he preached. He was closely connected to God and reflected the goodness of God to others. He had power but only used that power on behalf of others. He fed the hungry, healed the sick, made the broken whole, and set the oppressed free. No wonder people followed him!

If we are going to make disciples of Jesus, we first need to become more like Jesus. We need to take an honest look at ourselves and ask the question: Do people want my life? We are not asking if people envy our possessions or our paycheck. We are asking if they would want to experience the kind of life I am living. The life people truly long for is the abundant life that only Jesus can offer. When we call people into discipleship, we are calling them to follow the part of us that is like Jesus, not the parts that aren't. The more we are filled with the Holy Spirit, and the more we allow Jesus' presence within to make us more like him, the greater our disciple-making effectiveness will become.

Part of the reason people followed Jesus was because of who he is; another part was because of who they were. Some people were more open to Jesus than others. Jesus focused his life on these people. The religious leaders were deeply threatened by Jesus, and thus they were not very receptive to his teaching or his leadership. As you read the Gospels, you will notice Jesus did not spend much time intentionally hanging out with these religious leaders. Instead he spent most of his time with the ordinary peasants of Galilee and even with those who were considered sinners by the religious establishment. Jesus' strategy was simple and clear: focus on the people who are receptive and invest your life in them. As he said it, *"I was sent only to the lost sheep of the house of Israel"* (Matthew 15:24).

When Jesus trained the disciples to go out and identify these lost sheep on their own and call them to follow, he said, *"Whatever house you enter, first say, 'Peace be to this house!' And if a son of peace is there, your peace will rest upon him. But if not, it will return to you. And remain in the same house, eating and drinking what they provide, for a laborer deserves his wages. Do not go from house to house. Whenever you enter a town and they receive you, eat what is set before you."* (Luke 10:5-8) We refer to these receptive people Jesus taught us to look for as People of Peace.

Peace in biblical culture and language simply means hello. Jesus is telling us to go out, greet people warmly, and extend a hand of friendship to those we meet. Wherever that friendship is received and reciprocated, we are to invest in those relationships. Spend time with them. Eat with them. Share life with them. This is the beginning of discipleship. We are to identify People of Peace and build relationships with them. At that point Jesus says we are to "Heal the sick who are there and tell them, 'The kingdom of God has come near to you.'" (Luke 10:9)

Conversely, Jesus instructs us not to invest heavily in those who are not People of Peace to us: "But whenever you enter a town and they do not receive you, go into its streets and say, 'Even the dust of your town that clings to our feet we wipe off against you. Nevertheless know this, that the kingdom of God has come near.'" (Luke 10:10-11) This is not meant to be offensive or rude—it's just a clear boundary. Focus on those who are receptive to you, build relationships with them, and then show them what following Jesus looks like. This is how Jesus found his disciples. It's how he taught his disciples to find theirs. It's how we are to find ours.

MAKING DISCIPLES

Discipleship is a relationship and a journey. When Jesus invited his disciples to follow him, he began by telling them about the New Covenant and then showed them what a Covenant relationship looks like. He explained the Kingdom and then modeled Kingdom life for them. As they responded to his call, Jesus invited them to participate with him in his mission. When he fed the crowd of five thousand, Jesus asked the disciples to distribute food to the crowd. They got to be part of the powerful thing God was doing through Jesus. Then Jesus sent them out on their own mission so they could give it a try themselves. But he didn't send them out empty-handed. Jesus trained them, cheered them on, and was there to celebrate when they returned. Finally the day came when Jesus told them that he was going away and that they would continue this Kingdom work in the power of his Spirit. The process of discipleship was complete—they had learned to do what Jesus did. We all know the rest of the story.

The way we become like Jesus is by living in relationship with someone who can show us the kind of life Jesus lived. First we receive the information we need to understand from them. Then we begin to imitate the example they set for us. After this we are ready to innovate the specific way God is calling us to follow Jesus and make disciples.

We can picture these stages of the discipling process using the Discipling Triangle[6]:

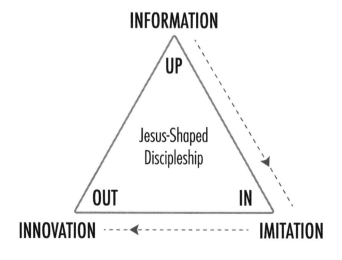

As we consider our call to make disciples, it makes sense that we would follow Jesus' example. By definition disciples will learn to do it the way Jesus did. This means that if we are disciples of Jesus, we will follow these same steps with others. We begin by explaining the information of the Good News of the Kingdom. Then we demonstrate what we are talking about through concrete actions. We invite our disciples to begin imitating our imperfect example. As they grow in skill and faith, we give them more and more opportunity until they are able to do what we have learned to do. Then we release them to innovate this way of life with others in their own unique context.

This is how Jesus did it, and it's how we are called to do it. Answering the invitation to join a small, accountable Huddle will provide a rich environment for you to begin to follow Jesus and to learn how to do the things he did. Forming and leading a Huddle of your own is a powerful way to answer the call to multiply disciples. This is what Jesus invited us into when he said Come follow me, and this is what he sent us to do when he said Go make disciples.

REFLECT, DISCUSS, AND RESPOND

1. How would it affect you to be in a group where others were helping you become more like Jesus by regularly repenting and believing?

2. Who are you investing your life in? Does anybody want your life? Who do you think might be a Person of Peace to you?

3. What do you think God might be saying to you right now?

4. What do you think God might want you to do in response to what he is saying?

part 3

WHO IS
YOUR FAMILY?

10

Rediscovering Family

THE BEST TIME OF YEAR

I was born in the same northwestern Montana town as my father and grandfather. Both my parents grew up in that town. My grandparents on both sides still lived in that town when I was a kid, along with numerous great aunts and uncles, cousins and second cousins. You get the idea. To say I have roots there is an understatement. However, I did not actually grow up in Montana. My dad was a naval pilot who took a job flying for Pan American Airlines, and so we lived in places like Hong Kong and West Berlin when I was a

kid. But no matter where in the world we lived, every summer we made our way back to the family cabin on the eastern shore of Flathead Lake, near that same northwestern Montana town. In fact, that is where I am writing this right now!

My grandfather bought lakefront property at Flathead Lake at the end of World War II and built a little two-bedroom cabin on it. My dad spent his childhood summers there. I spent every summer of my childhood there. Our sons have done the same all their lives, and we hope it will be so for generations to come. Since before I can remember, this was the place where my small family of four would suddenly swell to dozens of grandparents, aunts, uncles, cousins, and lifelong friends.

Summer with extended family at the lake was always the best time of the year. We gathered for meals around a dining table augmented by card tables and folding chairs. We would picnic, fish, hike, waterski, play cards, and roast marshmallows over beach fires. The time was filled with conversation, laughter, reports of recent events, and memories of times gone by. But before we knew it, vacation was over, and we scattered to different places where we resumed our "normal" lives.

Something was different and wonderful about being part of a big extended family, even for just a week or two. There was always someone to talk to or play with. You got to interact with a wide variety of personality types. Multiple generations brought both wisdom and passion to each other. Lots of hands helped fix the meals and clean up afterward. When problems arose there were plenty of people to help solve them. The joy and love seemed to multiply when we were all together. Of course, there were conflicts as well, but somehow the larger extended family seemed to be able to overcome whatever challenges it faced.

A BIBLICAL VISION OF FAMILY

What do you think of when you hear the word family? Most of us in the modern western world picture a mom, a dad, and some kids living in a single-family dwelling like a house or apartment. A nuclear family. A modern family. But it has not always been this way. In the Bible, and in many cultures around the world still today, family means grandparents, aunts, uncles, parents, brothers, sisters, cousins, close friends, and business partners, sharing life and working together in a multi-room house around an open courtyard. In the Bible this understanding of family is described by the Hebrew word *beth* and the Greek word *oikos*. These words are hard to translate because we don't have the same concept in English. They are often translated house or household, but those words make most modern people think of a nuclear family living in a single-family dwelling. That's not what these words mean.

For biblical people the primary expression of family was not the nuclear family, but the extended family, the *oikos*. To be honest, no one in the ancient world would be naïve enough to try making it with just a nuclear family! If their family had only one couple with kids, who would staff the family business? If the parents got sick, who would bring in the crops? If bandits attacked, who would fight them off? When the parents got old, who would care for them? Instinctively they knew they needed a larger family to face and overcome the inevitable challenges that would come. They knew the larger and stronger their *oikos* was, the more likely they were to be fruitful and prosperous.

The biblical *beth* or *oikos* was normally built around a common family business.

> In the Bible, and in many cultures around the world still today, family means grandparents, aunts, uncles, parents, brothers, sisters, cousins, close friends, and business partners, sharing life and working together in a multi-room house around an open courtyard.

Multiple generations working together in a common vocation could be very successful. For instance, the family business of Simon and Andrew in Capernaum was fishing. Simon and Andrew probably didn't live in separate houses and kiss their wives goodbye each morning as they went off to work somewhere carrying their lunchboxes. On the contrary, they likely shared the same extended family home, one where multiple generations lived and worked together in a common business. Some knotted nets. Some fashioned weights and floats. Some cleaned the fish and dried them on the rooftops. Some sold the fish in the marketplace. And some went out in the boats to catch the fish.

The biblical-era *oikos* existed for two primary reasons: provision and protection. In our modern world, we have developed various systems and structures that have led to the assumption we don't need an *oikos*. The industrial revolution led to the rise of corporations that replaced the family business, taking parents out of the home to fulfill their vocation. As people moved from villages and farms into rapidly growing cities, police forces and fire departments developed to maintain order and protect citizens from disaster. We now pay for things like health insurance, auto insurance, homeowner's insurance, life insurance, workers' compensation, and disability to protect ourselves from the inevitable challenges life continues to dish out.

All of this has led us to assume we can thrive with just a nuclear family or even as individuals. Casting off the provision and protection of the *oikos*, we look to modern social structures to provide what we need. One glance at the modern nuclear family might cause us to reassess this assumption. With over 50 percent of marriages ending in divorce and record numbers of single parents struggling to raise healthy kids in even less than a nuclear family, it is obvious our modern redefinition of family has put an unbearable strain on what has always been the cornerstone of human community.

This is not to say our modern support structures are to blame, but simply to say they are not enough to replace the strength and health of the extended family. What a blessing to have the protection of faithful police officers and firefighters! What a blessing to receive insurance funds to rebuild a home after it burns to the ground! But no insurance policy or civic organization can replace the relational resources provided by multiple generations of people who live and work together for a common good. Perhaps it is time for us to reconsider our assumptions about the family, not just for a week or two on summer vacation or every few years at a family reunion. Perhaps we need to rediscover a new kind of family that has been lost to the modern world.

JESUS' FAMILY

One of the challenges we face when reading the Bible is the inevitable effect that our unconscious cultural filters exert on how we understand its meaning. For instance, as a western American I have grown up with an intensely individualistic mindset. As a result, for most of my life, when I read the Gospels I automatically thought of Jesus primarily as an individual facing his challenges alone. I didn't think much about Jesus as part of a family. When I read of Jesus' baptism in the Jordan River, I missed the fact that John the Baptist was a relative of Jesus. When I read of Jesus preaching in his hometown synagogue, I never thought of his extended family being there. We can't eliminate our cultural filters, but we can become aware of them, adjust our perspective accordingly, and discover what we have been missing.

According to Luke, when Jesus began his public ministry, he returned to his hometown of Nazareth. Where would Jesus stay? Luke doesn't specify because it is assumed in that culture Jesus would return to his *oikos* and stay in one of the rooms in his extended family home. The Gospels tell us Jesus' family business was that of the tekton.

> Perhaps it is time for us to reconsider our assumptions about the family, not just for a week or two on summer vacation or every few years at a family reunion. Perhaps we need to rediscover a new kind of family that has been lost to the modern world.

This Greek word is often translated carpenter, and those of us with north-ern European cultural filters naturally envision Joseph and Jesus working with the lathe and plane in a woodshop. However, in a Middle Eastern context tekton is better translated builder, so we should think of the family as contractors who worked primarily in stone. Jesus and his brothers were strong men used to cutting, carrying, and setting blocks of limestone.

Luke tells us Jesus went to his hometown synagogue on the Sabbath day, and we know he would have gone with his aunts and uncles, mother and brothers and sisters, cousins, and anyone else who was living and working as part of that extended family. So when Jesus stood up to read from the scroll of the Prophet Isaiah, we can picture his *oikos* in the synagogue with him, excited for this moment when their family member was being rec-ognized as a rabbi by the whole village. Jesus read the powerful messianic promises from Isaiah 61, sat down in the teachers' seat, and dramatically declared, *"Today this Scripture has been fulfilled in your hearing"* (Luke 4:21).

At first the people in the synagogue marveled at his gracious words and began whispering their admiration and affirmation to each other. But Jesus went on to shock them by saying these blessings were not just for the Jew-ish people, but also for the pagan Gentiles who had been oppressing Jews for generations. This was too much to take! Centuries of anger, resentment, and bitterness erupted in rage, and the people dragged Jesus to one of the cliffs that drop into the Jezreel Valley to the south of Nazareth. They were preparing to throw him off. More than mob violence, this was a deliberate act of execution for heresy.

Again, my individualistic filters kept me from asking the obvious question: Where was Jesus' *oikos* while this is happening? Knowing that *oikos* is about provision and protection, shouldn't Jesus' stonemason uncles, brothers, and cousins be standing up for him, ready to fight? Why wasn't his mother clinging to his legs screaming for them not to hurt her son? At the very least, his family members were complicit in rejecting Jesus and his vision for the Good News of the Kingdom. Jesus had come to his own *oikos* to support his mission, and they utterly rejected him. John describes it this way: *"He came to his own, and his own people did not receive him"* (John 1:11). It is hard to imagine the depth of pain and disappointment he must have felt.

A NEW KIND OF FAMILY

After describing Jesus' mysterious escape from the crowd, Luke tells us Jesus went down to Capernaum, the prosperous fishing town on the north shore of the Sea of Galilee. Why did he go there? In John's account of Jesus' baptism, we hear about five guys from Galilee who showed great interest in Jesus and exhibited a desire to follow him—the brothers Simon and Andrew, Philip, Nathaniel, and an unnamed disciple (probably John). Simon, Andrew, and John were fishermen from Capernaum. Jesus went to Capernaum to find out if these guys were People of Peace to him would answer the call to discipleship. After teaching in the synagogue and delivering a possessed man, Luke tells us Jesus went with Simon and Andrew to their nearby extended family house—their *oikos*.

Archaeologists have identified, with almost complete certainty, the home of Simon and Andrew in Capernaum. It was comprised of eight rooms built around an open courtyard and surrounded by a secure wall. In that wall there was an outer gate that opened into the courtyard, and each room around the courtyard had a door and multiple windows opening into the courtyard. In one corner of the courtyard was a clay oven, and in another a set of stairs leading to the rooftop. This is where Simon and his wife and children lived, along with his brother Andrew's family, his wife's parents, and others who were close to them. This is where they slept at night, cooked and ate meals together, and carried out a prosperous fishing business that afforded them a large home in the prime neighborhood of their city.

When Jesus entered this *oikos* he discovered Simon's mother-in-law was sick, so he healed her. Then he shared in the meal she cooked for them. Next Jesus did something completely revolutionary: *"Now when the sun was setting, all those who had any who were sick with various diseases brought them to him, and he laid his hands on every one of them and healed them. And demons also came out of many, crying, 'You are the Son of God!' But he rebuked them and would not allow them to speak, because they knew that he was the Christ."* (Luke 4:40-41)

Remember, *oikos* was designed to provide for and protect the extended family. The *oikos* existed for the sake of the *oikos*. So Jesus was doing something completely unexpected—turning the family inside out! The door to the courtyard, which was meant to keep out anyone who was not part of the extended family, was flung wide open to invite everyone in—even the demon possessed! The message Jesus proclaimed in Nazareth was coming to fruition in Capernaum. The oppressed were set free. The blind received their sight. The Kingdom of God was coming! And it was all happening within a new kind of family—a family on mission.

> Jesus was doing something completely unexpected—turning the family inside out! The door to the courtyard, which was meant to keep out anyone who was not part of the extended family, was flung wide open to invite everyone in—even the demon possessed!

From this point on, the extended family of Simon and Andrew is described as Jesus' own *oikos*. Repeatedly the Gospel writers described Jesus' return to Capernaum as him coming home. Again and again we read of Jesus teaching, healing, and delivering people in the extended family home of Simon and Andrew, which was now his home and family. To make this absolutely clear, all three Synoptic Gospels describe what happened when Jesus' biological family heard rumors he had gone out of his mind. They came to the house of Simon and Andrew in Capernaum to bring him back to the *oikos* in Nazareth. In Mark's words, "And his mother and his brothers came, and standing outside they sent to him and called him. And a crowd was sitting around him, and they said to him, 'Your mother and your brothers are outside, seeking you.' And he answered them, 'Who are my mother and my brothers?' And looking about at those who sat around him, he said, 'Here are my mother and my brothers! For whoever does the will of God, he is my brother and sister and mother.'" (Mark 3:31-34)

Jesus was not a lone individual facing the challenges of extending God's Kingdom by himself. Jesus did not call his disciples to abandon their families in order to follow him. Quite the contrary, Jesus built a whole new kind of family and invited his followers to carry out his mission as part of that kind of *oikos*. This new kind of family was not defined primarily by blood or birth, but by Covenant relationship with God and Kingdom mission for the world. This new kind of family did not exist primarily to defend and provide for its own members, but to seek and save the lost. It was not a nuclear family, but an extended family. It was not only a biological family, but also a spiritual family. It was not a family that existed exclusively for itself, but a family that existed for others. It was a Kingdom family—a family on mission.

REFLECT, DISCUSS, AND RESPOND

1. How does Jesus' definition of family compare to your patterns of family life?

2. What would change if your family were to explicitly identify a mission greater than itself?

3. What do you think God might be saying to you right now?

4. What do you think God might want you to do in response to what he is saying?

11

Building a Family on Mission

A FAMILY BUSINESS

By working together, the extended families of Simon and Andrew, as well as those of James and John, had built successful family businesses. Imagine their surprise when Jesus offered to take their *oikos* businesses to a whole new level! Luke tells us how Jesus borrowed Simon's fishing boat to use as a floating pulpit and then gave these professional fishermen some free advice: *"Put out into the deep and let down your nets for a catch."* After hauling in the net-splitting catch of a lifetime, the four fishermen were overwhelmed with amazement. Jesus made them a unique family business proposition: *"'Do not be afraid; from now on you will be catching men.' And when they had brought their boats to land, they left everything and followed him."* (Luke 5:1-11)

Jesus entered the *oikos* of Simon and Andrew and showed them how to build a whole new kind of family by opening the door and inviting in the lost and the broken. Now he was telling these fishermen that this new kind of family was going to develop a whole new kind of business by going out after a more important catch. No longer would they simply be going after fish; now catching people was going to be their goal. The family business was to become the mission of God. Later in his ministry, when Jesus entered the *oikos* of a tax collector named Zacchaeus and transformed his family business, Jesus was crystal clear about the purpose of his mission: *"For the Son of Man came to seek and to save the lost"* (Luke 19:10). Jesus was showing us how to move a family beyond self-serving protection and provision into a purpose far greater.

WHAT KIND OF FAMILY?

When Pam and I were married, we knew God was not calling us to choose between our family or our mission. Our desire was to do both well. We believed God was calling us to build a strong marriage and healthy family while at the same time building a healthy, Kingdom-advancing church. The problem was that these goals often seemed at odds with each other. To protect our family from the often-overwhelming demands of leading a church, Pam had to develop a strong firewall between our home and our ministry to protect our family from our mission.

But this approach had unwanted effects. By compartmentalizing our lives into family and mission, Pam and I often ended up feeling pulled in two different directions. Resentment tended to accumulate in both directions.

> Jesus was showing us how to move a family beyond self-serving protection and provision into a purpose far greater.

Although Pam had always been an active leader in the church, she found herself more focused on family, while I was more focused on our mission. These two callings always seemed to drive us apart rather than bring us together. Whenever we achieved what seemed like a good balance, it only took one unexpected challenge to knock us off balance and pit our mission against our family once again.

As we began the journey of discipleship, we noticed something very different about the families of the people from whom we were learning. Their lives did not seem to be compartmentalized the way ours was. They had a natural kind of integration we had not seen before. They didn't have one way of being a family and another way of carrying out their mission. They didn't seem pulled in different directions trying to keep both these balls in the air at the same time. They weren't trying to walk the tightrope of balance by guarding their boundaries. Instead they had healthy rhythms of rest and work that resulted in good fruit. They had strong marriages and healthy kids, but they were also highly effective in carrying out their mission. They weren't perfect, but we liked their way of life better than ours.

Gradually we began to emulate this way of life and learned how to integrate our lives rather than compartmentalize. Instead of setting up a firewall between our family and our mission, we began to see our family was meant to be at the heart of our mission. Instead of constantly trying to achieve a fragile balance, we learned to establish predicable patterns that built up momentum that could be maintained even when the unexpected happened. We have come to understand we don't have to choose between family OR mission. We don't have to try to balance family AND mission. Instead, we are learning how to become a family ON mission.[7]

family **OR** mission

family **AND** mission

family **ON** mission

PUTTING IDEAS INTO ACTION

Jesus said those who hear his word and act on it are like the wise man who built his *oikos* on the rock. So we began to act in faith on the things we felt Jesus was saying to us. The first thing we did was begin growing our nuclear family into an extended family. Most of our married life, our home was somewhat of a fortress—a place where we retreated to escape the pressures of ministry. Now we began to open the doors of our home and our lives and invite people in, starting with the people we were discipling.

> Instead of setting up a firewall between our family and our mission, we began to see our family was meant to be at the heart of our mission.

Following the example of families we saw who were on mission together, we learned to keep things lightweight and low maintenance so it did not put undue stress on anyone. We started gathering every other Sunday after church to build a stronger sense of extended family. Everyone brought food to share, and we spent some time sharing encouragement and praying together. If we were going to the movies or to the beach or out to dinner, we included those who were becoming part of our extended spiritual family. It didn't happen overnight, but by listening to God, following the example of those who were mentoring us, and being accountable to concrete steps of faith, gradually we developed our own *oikos*.

The next step was identifying our Kingdom family business. We had lived in the same neighborhood for about twelve years, but the only neighbors we knew were those who went to our church. I was deeply convicted that I had been ignoring the lost people in my own neighborhood. God showed us that our mission field was the block we lived on. We began to make room in our lives to befriend our neighbors. We started spending more time in our front yard, not just the backyard. We looked for ways to serve those on our block and became better neighbors to them. I started baby-sitting for one over-worked couple a few doors down. We invited three couples that seemed to be receptive and positive People of Peace over for dinner. Pretty soon we got invitations to several of the kids' birthday parties. Before long we noticed neighbors going out of their way to talk with us and even serve us.

As we built relationships with neighbors who were not people of faith or active in a faith community, we began to connect them with our growing spiritual family. We walked our neighborhood in prayer, listening to what God was saying to us about serving and reaching our neighbors. About once a month, we started planning events we thought our unbelieving or unchurched neighbors and friends would enjoy. At Christmas we baked cookies and delivered them to neighbors while caroling, just to let them know we cared. In the summer we gathered for picnics in the nearby park and organized simple games for the kids. We gathered items for a yard sale and gave the proceeds to a family in the neighborhood that was struggling with medical bills. We looked for any way we could serve our neighbors and invite them into our new spiritual family.

We didn't see massive conversions or immediate revival break out in our neighborhood, but in time we saw lives changed by the power of God's love working through an extended spiritual family on mission together. We had opportunities to make a practical difference in the lives of people who really needed help. Over the course of a couple of years, we saw a number of people come to faith in Jesus. Some ended up joining our church. Some connected with other churches. We are still learning how to live as a family on mission, and it is both challenging and rewarding to this day.

HEALTHY RHYTHMS

Some people, when they first hear about building a family on mission, feel overwhelmed. Their schedule is already so full that they can't imagine inviting more people into their life or their home. Some people, particularly those who are naturally introverted, are afraid all their energy will be drained by being around lots of people all the time. To them, integrating family with mission sounds like boundary violations of the worst kind.

But when we look at Jesus' life, we can see he lived with very intentional and healthy rhythms. Early in the morning, while it was still dark, Jesus withdrew to a lonely place to spend time alone with his heavenly Father. From that place of abiding and rest, Jesus then stepped into the busy, fruitful life of ministry he was living. Every Sabbath day Jesus gathered with others at the synagogue for worship and rest with his extended family. After some days of healing the sick and declaring the Good News of the Kingdom, Jesus took his disciples away to a peaceful place to rest for a while. Once in a while Jesus took the disciples away on a longer retreat, to an area where no one would even recognize them, so they could have an extended period of rest.

As Jesus' notoriety grew, there was tremendous pressure exerted on him to perform and countless demands on his time, but it did not overwhelm him. Because Jesus lived with these intentional rhythms of rest and work, he was able to respond appropriately to the needs of so many while still maintaining a healthy lifestyle.

THE VINE AND THE BRANCHES

In addition to his living example, Jesus gave us an amazing picture of how to live with healthy and fruitful rhythms: *"I am the vine; you are the branches. Whoever abides in me and I in him, he it is that bears much fruit, for apart from me you can do nothing"* (John 15:5).

Jesus was comparing the connection between the main grape vine and its branches with the Covenantal relationship that makes us one with him. Just as the main trunk of the vine provides everything the branch needs to grow and become fruitful, we can depend on Jesus for everything we need to live the abundant and fruitful Kingdom life for which we are created. The crucial factor in living out that Kingdom life is the Covenantal connection between Jesus and us. If the branch is not deeply woven into the fiber of the vine, it will not receive the nutrients it needs to flourish and become fruitful. If that branch stays connected to the vine it will naturally grow and produce good fruit. Jesus says the same is true of us.

LEARNING JESUS' RHYTHMS

Pam and I have always struggled with the busy pace of life and ministry. Once we were around people who were intentionally living according to the rhythms of Jesus, we saw how much better this pattern is than always trying to police boundaries and seek elusive balance. The people who were discipling us had a daily rhythm of reading the Scriptures and praying, both by themselves and as a family. They also scheduled intentional days and seasons for abiding and rest. Out of these times of abiding, they moved into fruitful Kingdom work. They described it as a rhythm of swinging from rest and abiding into work and fruitfulness, and then back again.

Gradually Pam and I started to develop these same kinds of rhythms in our lives. Instead of reading our own Scriptures, we decided to get on the same Bible reading plan. We started listening to a daily online devotional based on those same Scripture readings. We both became a lot more consistent in spending time with the Father each day, because we could support each other in establishing that daily rhythm. We also found we started to share with each other and pray together more regularly about what God was saying to us and what we

> Because Jesus lived with these intentional rhythms of rest and work, he was able to respond appropriately to the needs of so many while still maintaining a healthy lifestyle.

felt he wanted us to do. Now we find that reading God's Word and pray-ing about it together is as natural each morning as brushing our teeth and eating breakfast.

We began to seek healthier rhythms in other areas of our lives as well. Jesus said fruitful branches are the ones the Vinegrower prunes so they will pro-duce more and better fruit. So we began to submit to the Father's pruning in our lives, allowing him to clean out some of the things that were good, but not necessary, to make room for the new things he wanted to do. We found this allowed us more time to disciple leaders, to invite people into our lives, and to learn how to live a missional life in our neighborhood.

We also started to practice a full 24-hour Sabbath day each week. From Friday night until Saturday night, we only did things we wanted to do. We went out on Friday night. Slept in on Saturday morning. Had breakfast in our pajamas. I might go surfing. Pam might putter in the garden. We might sit out on the patio reading books or the Bible. Took a walk. Went for a bike ride. Visited friends. We got to do whatever would help us rest, recharge, and reconnect with the Father and one another. I found myself looking forward to and excited about our weekly days of rest.

We began to look at our calendar differently. Instead of scheduling things however they came up, we identified periods of rest that we would protect in between the busy periods of fruitful activity we knew God was calling us to do. Sometimes these abiding seasons included times to get away for a weekend or a longer vacation, but they also came with a mindset that we would cut back and make more room for rest and abiding during those weeks. This helped us be ready for the seasons we knew were going to be more demanding, and helped us engage in fruitful activity with greater ef-fectiveness and joy.

We are still learning this way of life, but today the rhythm of abiding and fruitfulness comes much more naturally for us. There is a momentum that builds when you establish these kinds of rhythms in your life. Even when unexpected things come your way, you can still swing right back into those rhythms. The rhythm of Jesus' life of abiding and bearing fruit is like a flywheel that keeps us following in his footsteps even when unexpected challenges arise.

A PICTURE OF HEALTHY RHYTHMS

Just as Jesus used visual images familiar to the people of his time, such as lilies of the field and birds of the air, we use images to help people in our day to remember, practice, and pass on the principles Jesus taught and modeled for his disciples. We can picture the rhythms of Jesus' life as a semicircle, the shape created by a pendulum swinging back and forth from one side to the other[8]:

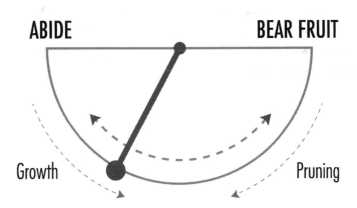

The Semicircle gives us a picture of Jesus' rhythm of swinging from restful abiding into fruitful work and then back again on a daily, weekly, seasonal, and annual basis. When we get stuck over in fruitful work too long and can't seem to get back to abiding, the Semicircle reminds us we need to submit to the Father's pruning. Likewise, when we have spent enough time abiding, the Father produces growth in us that leads to more and better fruitfulness.

As you begin to make disciples and build an extended spiritual family that is on mission together, you will find healthy rhythms are what make this way of life possible and sustain the fruitfulness of a missional *oikos*. Families on mission make intentional space for abiding on a daily, weekly, seasonal, and annual basis. We found the process of pruning and establishing healthy rhythms gave us time to invest in people's lives and invite them into our family, while still giving us more time for rest and renewal. These rhythms of pruning, abiding, growth, and fruitfulness will help you build a healthy family on mission as you follow Jesus together.

REFLECT, DISCUSS, AND RESPOND

1. What would it look like for you to build a family on mission?

2. How do your rhythms of life compare to Jesus' rhythms?

3. What do you think God might be saying to you right now?

4. What do you think God might want you to do in response to what he is saying?

12

Facing the Challenge Together

IN NEED OF TRAINING WHEELS

I vividly remember the Christmas morning I watched my son Bobby pedal off on his first two-wheeled bicycle. He had mastered the stable trike, but now it was time for the freedom and thrill of two wheels. Or almost time. While assembling the bike, I was sure to bolt two training wheels on his back axle. You know how training wheels work. They ride just a little higher than the back tire. As the bike tips one way or the other, the training wheels help stabilize and keep the bike upright.

I ran alongside at first, helping him get the feel, but now he was on his own.

As Bobby rode out into the great expanse of the cul-de-sac where we lived, I saw him begin to tip to the left. Then the left training wheel caught him and pushed him back to the right. He held the line for a couple more pedals, and then the bike lurched to the right, but the right training wheel did its job and kept him from crashing.

It's great to have training wheels in place when you are learning a skill as tricky as riding a bike. The same is true when we are learning something as challenging as building a missional family. In Jesus' time no one needed to learn how to live as an *oikos*, because that was the naturally inherited way of life. In our culture we have largely lost the memory of extended family, so we have a lot to learn if we are going to follow the way of Jesus. Most of us don't know how to build a family business, so embracing the Father's Kingdom business in our family will take some training. We need enough structure in place that we can learn what it looks like to do mission as an extended family in our context, and also enough freedom that we can grow into an authentic missional *oikos*. We need a set of training wheels just far enough off the ground so we can try out this missional way of life without crashing.

We use a vehicle called a Missional Community that serves as training wheels for building a family on mission. A Missional Community is meant to help us learn how to live as an extended spiritual family on mission together. A Missional Community is a mid-sized group of people who are living UP-IN-OUT lives together. They have a Covenant commitment to one another as a spiritual family and a Kingdom calling from God to serve and reach the lost. They spend time together learning how to listen to God, building one another up in love, and seeking to connect with those who are far from God. A Missional Community is larger than a small group and smaller than a worship service. We like to say they are small enough to care, but large enough to dare. They normally meet outside the church, gather around meals, and have a clearly defined focus for their mission.[9] Simply put, a Missional Community is a houseful of friends on a mission.

EVERYBODY GETS TO PLAY

As we have seen, in biblical times extended families were built around a family business in which everyone played a part. If it was an *oikos* of shepherds, some members of the family would herd the sheep and goats, some would milk them, some would tend to their health, some would shear them, some would bundle and transport the wool, some would spin wool into yarn, some would weave garments, and so on. Everyone played a critical role in the success of the family business. The same is true of the family on mission.

> A Missional Community is a mid-sized group of people who are living UP-IN-OUT lives together.

One of the great things about Missional Communities is they provide an environment where everyone gets to participate in the life and mission of the Body of Christ. Too often in our typical church gatherings, only those with certain levels of skill or knowledge get to take an active part in the spiritual life of the community. The singers sing, the readers read, the preachers preach, the prayers pray, and the announcers announce. Most of us are left on the sidelines watching. In contrast to this, Paul described the church as a human body and emphasized how every part is critical to the health of the whole. He specified five critical roles within the body that help us grow up into the fullness of Christ and strengthen his Body the Church. When writing to churches in Asia Minor, Paul said, *"Grace was given to each one of us according to the measure of Christ's gift… And he gave the apostles, the prophets, the evangelists, the shepherds and teachers, to equip the saints for the work of ministry, for building up the body of Christ."* (Ephesians 4:7, 11-12)

In a Missional Community all the members have the opportunity to grow in their gifting as they learn to serve and lead. Everyone gets to grow as a servant by bringing food to share, serving the meals, and helping to clean up afterward. Everyone gets to grow as an apostle as we discern the new ways God is calling us to fulfill our unique missional calling. Everyone gets to grow as a prophet when we spend time listening for what God is saying and sharing with each other encouraging words and pictures. Everyone gets to grow as an evangelist when we go out and find ways to connect with our People of Peace. Everyone gets to grow as a shepherd when we pray for each other and comfort those who are hurting in our midst. Everyone gets to grow as a teacher when we discuss God's Word and how to put it into practice.

Not only are there roles for everyone, but there is also a place for every kind of person in a Missional Community. Jesus specifically chose twelve men to be part of his inner circle of disciples, but he opened the door of the *oikos* in Capernaum to everyone who would come—even the demon possessed! Huddles are a vehicle for discipling leaders, and as such only certain people are invited into a given Huddle. However, everyone is invited into a Missional Community. There is a place for people who know nothing about Jesus or the Bible, and also for those who have been walking with Jesus their entire lives. There is a place for men and women of every kind of background, economic status, racial heritage, educational level, and vocational identity. Missional Communities are healthiest when they are multigenerational, just like extended families are. There is a place for old people, young people, babies, parents, teens, middle-aged people, and everyone in between. Missional Communities are great fun because everyone gets to play!

MISSIONAL RHYTHMS

Just as Jesus demonstrated a healthy rhythm of abiding and bearing fruit, he also showed us how to live in healthy three-dimensional rhythms of UP, IN, and OUT.

UP   Jesus was always in close communion with his heavenly Father. He simply did what he saw the Father doing and spoke the words the Father gave him to speak.

IN Sometimes Jesus focused on his relationship with the twelve disciples. He took them away by themselves for times of teaching, training, and abiding.

OUT Other times Jesus focused on their mission (OUT). He welcomed the outcast into their *oikos* in Capernaum and healed the broken. He took the houseful of disciples out on the highways and byways to seek and save the lost.

As we learn how to build missional families, it is important to develop the same kind of rhythms in our Missional Communities.

Practically, this means Jesus-shaped Missional Communities will establish a regular rhythm of gatherings that focus on UP and IN, along with regular activities that focus on IN and OUT. For instance, our Missional Community typically gathers every other Sunday over lunch for an UP-IN time together. Everyone brings food to share, and after eating we share encouraging testimonies of the good things God is doing in our lives. Then we open it up for people to share some things God has been saying to them through their daily Bible reading. Then we break into groups of three to share personal prayer requests and pray for each other. This would be a typical UP-IN time together.

About once a month, we plan an IN-OUT activity aimed at helping our unbelieving or unchurched friends connect with our spiritual family. This could be as simple as a prayer walk in the neighborhood or hanging out in the front yard to meet people who are out and about. It could be going out to do random acts of kindness, like giving out water bottles at the beach,

> Jesus-shaped Missional Communities will establish a regular rhythm of gatherings that focus on UP and IN, along with regular activities that focus on IN and OUT.

or doing neighborhood cleanup or yard work. It could be raising money for those in need or offering practical support to someone who is struggling. It could be organizing a public event like a picnic and games in the park where everyone is invited. It could be a gathering in someone's home where people of peace are invited to come and join in the fun. The point of these kinds of IN-OUT activities is to find ways to identify those who are open to us, and then begin building relationships with them so they can encounter Jesus.

Building a spiritual family that is following the example of Jesus also means there will be seasons when the Missional Community takes a break from gathering for a period of time. Our Missional Communities typically take some weeks off in the summer, over Christmas and New Year's, and during the Easter holiday. These down times give the leaders an opportunity to rest and abide, giving space for vacations and holiday activities. These are critical rhythms for a healthy family on mission that wants to produce good fruit that lasts. The point of living as part of a Missional Community is not to make our lives more stressful, but more fruitful. There are sacrifices and challenging steps of faith we are called to make on this journey of building a family on mission, but when we remember that in God's Kingdom less can be more, it leads us into a more abundant life.

JESUS' BUILDING PROJECT

Ever since Adam and Eve made the fateful mistake of thinking they could live a better life without their Creator, God has been working to redeem and rebuild this broken world into a fruitful Kingdom of joy where his will is done on earth as it is in heaven. Jesus was born into an extended family of builders and stonemasons, but even as a boy he told his parents he had to be about his Father's business.

While on that retreat up north in Caesarea Philippi when Jesus gave Simon a new name, Jesus explained how his Kingdom building project would be accomplished: *"I tell you, you are Peter, and on this rock I will build my church, and the gates of hell shall not prevail against it"* (Matthew 16:18). Simon was now Peter, aka "Rocky." The implication is obvious: Jesus was not the only Rock in this building project. Jesus' plan to save the world is to use us to build his church. Jesus will do the building if we will offer our lives to him as the raw material by which God's great rebuilding project is accomplished.

Jesus came to fulfill the Father's great work of rebuilding a broken creation through his own life, death, and resurrection. Before his death Jesus quoted Psalm 118:22 and predicted the Father was going to carry out this building project in a very unexpected way: "Have you never read in the Scriptures: *'The stone that the builders rejected has become the cornerstone; this was the Lord's doing, and it is marvelous in our eyes?'"* (Matthew 21:42).

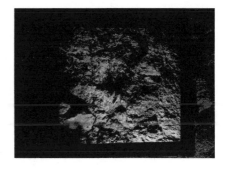

Archaeologists tell us the rock of Golgotha on which Jesus was crucified is actually a section of limestone which the fifth century BC rebuilders of the Temple quarried around because it was deeply cracked and fissured, leaving a large, rocky outcropping which looked like a skull. The place of Jesus' crucifixion is literally the stone that the builders rejected! On that very rock, Jesus was rejected by those who nailed him to the cross. But through his death and resurrection, he has become the cornerstone and has laid the foundation for the Father's work of redemption and restoration. By God's grace we now have the privilege of participating in the completion of this greatest of all building projects.

After many years of seeing Jesus building his church through ordinary people like himself, Peter expressed it this way to his disciples: *"As you come to him, a living stone rejected by men but in the sight of God chosen and precious, you yourselves like living stones are being built up as a spiritual house, to be a holy priesthood, to offer spiritual sacrifices acceptable to God through Jesus Christ"* (1 Peter 2:4-5).

The word we translate spiritual *house* here is literally spiritual *oikos*. We are the living stones Jesus is using to build extended families of disciples whose mission is to seek and save the lost. We are the holy priests who represent our Father and mediate his saving grace by welcoming the broken and outcast into our spiritual *oikos*, inviting them to follow us as we follow Jesus. We are the means by which Jesus will save the world and establish his eternal Kingdom. Our call is allowing Jesus to change us more into his image by teaching us how to live in a family on mission and how to multiply that way of life in the lives of others.

Jesus showed us what this abundant way of life looks like, and he is continuing to build his church by empowering us to live that life today. As we embrace our Covenant identity as sons and daughters of the heavenly Father, claiming the authority we have been given to represent our Daddy the King, he will give us the power we need to make disciples the way Jesus did and multiply families on mission who are doing the will of God on earth as it is in heaven. This is God's plan to change the world forever, and we get to be part of it!

YOUR INVITATION

Today there are followers of Jesus all over the world who are a part of a missional discipling movement that is seeking the way of life described in this book. We come from varied backgrounds and represent many different tribes. We are seeking to serve and reach people with the Gospel in myriads of cultural contexts through many different means. But we share a common vision to put Jesus-shaped discipleship back into the hands of ordinary people. We are seeking to build extended missional families that seek and save the lost. We are learning how to carry out this mission in the authority and power of Jesus. Our passion is to empower missional disciples.

If you have resonated with anything in this book, you might be tempted to think that, having read it, you are now ready to do it on your own. That would be to mistake information alone for discipleship! The truth is you can't get discipleship from a book, and you can't give away what you haven't received. We all need someone to imitate before we begin to innovate. If there is someone in your life or in your church who is already on this journey of discipleship and mission, ask them if you can go with them on that journey.

> As we embrace our Covenant identity as sons and daughters of the heavenly Father, claiming the authority we have been given to represent our Daddy the King, he will give us the power we need to make disciples the way Jesus did and multiply families on mission who are doing the will of God on earth as it is in heaven.

This is not an overnight process, it is a new way of life and a culture that will take years to develop. It begins with you, your spouse if you are married, your kids if you have kids, people you are close to, and then spreads to those you invite into an extended family. Those who try to do this on their own inevitably fail, and those who try to rush the process always end up regretting it. Reading this book is the first step in a long journey. We invite you to come and join us on this journey.

If you are looking for resources to help you learn this way of life, please visit our website at www.3dmovements.com. We offer various workshops and resources to help you on this journey. If you don't have someone to learn from who is already on this journey, joining an online 3DM Coaching Huddle is a great way to gain the tools you need to live this out in your daily life and home, at work, and in your neighborhood.

Building a discipling culture and multiplying families on mission in the power of the Spirit is not a quick or easy process, but we have found it is well worth whatever it costs. Jesus said we should count the cost before we answer his call to discipleship. If you feel the Spirit moving you, then come and find out more about what it means to join us on this adventure of empowering missional disciples.

REFLECT, DISCUSS, AND RESPOND

1. How would a Missional Community help you learn to live more effectively in a family on mission?

2. What is the next step for you to live a more Jesus-shaped life?

3. What do you think God might be saying to you right now?

4. What do you think God might want you to do in response to what he is saying?

END NOTES

[1]Breen, Mike. *Building a Discipling Culture*. Pawley's Island: 3DM Publishing, 2009. pp. 67-83.

[2]Breen, Mike. *Covenant and Kingdom The DNA of the Bible*. Pawley's Island: 3DM Publishing, 2010. p. 113.

[3]Neusner, Jacob, editor. *The Mishnah: A New Translation*. New Haven: Yale University, 1988. Avot 1:4

[4]Breen, Mike. *Choosing to Learn from Life*. Pawley's Island: 3DM Publishing, 2015.

[5]Breen, Mike. *Building a Discipling Culture*. Pawley's Island: 3DM Publishing, 2009. p. 18l

[6]Breen, Mike. B*uilding a Discipling Culture*. Pawley's Island: 3DM Publishing, 2009. p. 41

[7]For a practical guide to building a family on mission, see Breen, Mike and Sally. *Family on Mission*. Pawley's Island: 3DM Publishing, 2014.

[8]Breen, Mike. *Building a Discipling Culture*. Pawley's Island: 3DM Publishing, 2009. pp. 85-97.

[9]For more information on Missional Communities see Breen, Mike. *Leading Missional Communities*. Pawley's Island: 3DM Publishing, 2013.